THIS IS A WORK OF FICTION.
ANY SIMILARITY BETWEEN REAL
PERSONS, PLACES, OR THINGS, AND
THE FICTICIOUS PERSONS, PLACES,
OR THINGS PORTRAYED HEREIN,
IS ENTIRELY COINCIDENTAL.

Library of Congress
Copyright © 2015   John Regan
TXu 1-964-131

All rights reserved. No part of this book may be reproduced, stored in a retrieval system, transmitted in any form or by any means electronic or mechanical, including but not limited to photocopying, recording, or electronic file distribution, without the written prior permission of the author.

Published by John Regan, 2017
North Palm Beach, FL

ISBN: 978-0-692-61682-6

Order this book on line at:

www.Amazon.com

Or

For a signed copy

johnregan2100@gmail.com

jreganjr@protonmail.com

Free shipping

"Be prepared for surprises, wonders, and lots of soul-warming experiences from the very first chapter. THE MONK AND THE SKUNK definitely belongs in that rare category of "can't put it down" novels. And don't let the memorable animals you'll meet lull you into thinking this is just a children's book, even though the older kids will love it as much as us grownups! You may never forget Fragrance, or Lightning, or Target, or especially Aroma. And watch out-- you may very well change your lifestyle after finishing the final chapter of this compelling and charming novel."

Tom Sherry
 Author of A DESTINY TO DIE FOR

I read the Monk & The Skunk in only two days – It's a hard book to put down. John Regan is a great story teller and has a wonderful ability to keep the reader interested to the very end.

Don Kazimir
Respect Life Ministry Director
Catholic Charities, Diocese of Palm Beach

God created all things to love Him. The Skunk confirms what we already felt in our hearts. Animals must go to Heaven! The Monk and The Skunk gives us hope that we will live with animals in eternity!

Stephanie Munroe

I am happy to endorse "The Monk & the Skunk" by John Regan. This tale will appeal both to older children and to adults. In this day & age, we need to see the connection between all living creatures, & our Creator. This book does so in a very beguiling fashion. Buy it for yourself, your kids, & grandkids.

Jack land Ph. D. Child & Family Development, Syracuse University. Co-founder of the South County Mental Health Center, Delray Beach, Florida

_____

God's heavenly gate welcomes all of His creation, even His furry little ones.

Hope D'Alessandro Forte

_____

It's the type book you can read in one sitting but you don't want to as you enjoy it so much you don't want it to end.

Melanie Hill

_____

I have never questioned whether or not animals go to Heaven. I just knew. Animals are a little gift from God. There is no better sound than the beautiful birds to greet you in the morning and no better feeling than being welcomed by your faithful dog at the end of the day. Why would God leave them behind?

Faith Psillas

_____

I don't think of heaven as a "place". However: wherever, or whatever, or if ever, animals are of course welcome. All creatures great and small, as has been said, the great God made them all.

Anonymous

Are we the only ones in God's creation to go to Heaven? Do animals who have been loyal pets and friends to people simply perish? Possibly, but more than likely, their lives are honored. Jesus' resurrection as noted in all 4 Gospels sets the tone for all created things.

Eve R. Carr

There is no question in my mind, whatsoever, that animals definitely go to heaven. No question about it.

Ann Carroll

I believe animals go to heaven, because all of God's creation is worthy of that. Everything of this earth created in His image is a taste of what the beauty of heaven will be. Although heaven will surpass our worldly expectations of beauty, I think the gifts of this earth will be there. Animals are one of many gifts of this earth.

Taylor de Lacey

Like the temple veil that was torn in two when Jesus died, the veil of misunderstanding between the animals and us will be gone in Heaven. And they will tell us how much they loved us and needed our love in return.

D.W.

When God instructed Noah to put two of each kind of animal on the ark, He made it clear just how important the animals are in His plan of creation. Why would He then abandon them when they die? Surely, if He loves them on earth, He will love them in Heaven too.

Mary Ann

Being an avid animal lover all my life & an even more devout Pro-Lifer, I believe all animals go to Heaven... and, I have had every type of animal as a pet- including armadillos, ferrets, pot-bellied pigs, raccoons, snakes, opossums, cats, dogs and yes, even a skunk. I believe they all have souls and I know that I will see them all once again up in the Animal Kingdom in Heaven right alongside my all-time favorite saint, Saint Francis of Assisi... May they all rest in peace in the loving arms of their creator.

Willy Guardiola (willyguardiola@yahoo.com)
President
Christian on a Mission Non-Profit Ministry

Preface

Many years ago, while still a young boy, my Golden Retriever puppy was run over and killed by an automobile. I was devastated and wondered if I would ever see him again. A few years later several of my pigeons froze to death in my pigeon coop because I forgot to turn the heat on. I wondered if they too were permanently gone. Shortly thereafter I decided to free my prize pair of English Homing Pigeons which I had purchased and used for several years as breeders. The hope was to fill my pigeon coop with pure bred homers. During those few years it was necessary to keep them from returning to their place of birth, which is what homing pigeons do. To accomplish that, their wing feathers had to be carefully clipped. This would afford them the ability to fly within the coop but not escape to freedom. This had to be done with precision, making sure not to cut the main outer part of the wing, known as the arm, which would never grow back. Keeping the bird motionless, while clipping its wings, is very difficult. The slightest wrong move and the bird would never be able to fly again. Now that the time had come to let the birds return home, their clipped feathers had to be pulled out so new feathers could grow in. This would take several months of waiting until the new feathers had completely reformed the wings to their original shape. Once the pigeons were ready to fly again I took the larger male outside and released him. I had no idea where he was born, but I knew that he did and would fly directly home. This was a large and very powerful bird and he immediately flew straight up for several hundred feet and then began to fly in very tight circles while continuing to fly higher and higher. Several minutes later he had reached such a high altitude that he was barely visible. Suddenly, as if he had received a message, I was amazed to see him fly in a perfectly straight line, due east, with incredible speed. Large homing pigeons can reach speeds in excess of 90 miles per hour, and travel up to 700 miles in a single day. As I watched that amazing creature of God racing towards home, the recurring question surfaced in my mind; will I ever see him again?

One sunny winter day, not long after I was married, I decided to go deer hunting. The temperature was in the twenties as I headed into the woods. I knew there were deer in that particular vicinity as I had seen them on many occasions near the highway. The wind was from the northeast, and I was moving into their territory from the southwest which meant I was downwind from the animals. They would certainly not smell me and probably not hear me either. Ten minutes later, as I moved steadily north east, I suddenly stopped dead in my tracks. There on the ground, five feet in front of me, lay an entire family of white tailed deer. Steam rose from their bodies as they lay in a circle in the tall grass. For breathless seconds they stared at me and I stared back, paralyzed with indecision. Do I shoot them, or let them go? Suddenly, as if they had communicated in some unknown way, they jumped in unison to their feet and dashed away leaping over tall bushes. I raised the rifle to fire but could not bring myself to pull the trigger. I knew instinctively that those deer were individual persons. Not human persons, but still, they were individually somebody and I could not hurt or take their life from them. By the time I reached home a major decision had been made. Within the hour the rifle was destroyed and I never hunted again.

Fast forward twenty years and I'm with my teenage children spear fishing in 10 feet of water. I was accustomed to fishing with fishing poles but had never used a spear before. Suddenly a large school of fish passed right in front of me. They were about the size of a shoe. Immediately I speared one and pulled it toward me. When I pulled the spear out it left a huge hole in the side of the fish. Immediately the school disappeared. One fish, however, identical to the one I had speared, stayed with the now dead fish. Because everything looks bigger underwater, when I looked at the dead fish up close it wasn't any bigger than my hand. I decided to throw it away and as it started to sink to the bottom the other fish continually tried to push it back up to the surface. As it sank deeper and deeper the other fish eventually disappeared, probably realizing that it was a losing battle. That was the end of my spear fishing days. I had uselessly destroyed one of God's creatures.

Years later, while driving home, I noticed a Morning Dove lying on the road. Slowing down I could see it was trying to flap it wings but not having much success. I stopped, picked it up and brought it home, placing it in a closet where it would be safe. It had an injured wing and I hoped it would eventually heal. It did, and months later I released the bird and it flew away without incident. Somehow I sensed that the bird was grateful. It was somebody that was helped by someone else.

Recently, I was in the back yard and two Morning Doves were walking on the ground nearby. I have perfected the morning dove call and can imitate them fairly well. Usually they will respond, then I respond, then they respond, and it goes on for some time. This particular day the male walked closer to me and with a puffed out chest responded exactly to my call. I was able to mimic him almost perfectly. He stepped closer and imitated me again. I held my ground and imitated him. This went on for several minutes until he was about two feet from my shoes. He puffed out his chest and seemed almost irritated that I was daring to imitate him. He gave his call with a load vengeance and I suddenly realized that he must be stating his claim on his wife nearby, and I, he assumed, was competition. He was not a happy bird so I gave it up and he flew away.

Then there was the pelican with the fishing line wrapped around his wing and neck. Every time he tried to flap his wings he pulled on his neck and was immobilized as a result. We brought him into the house, and my wife and children and I untangled the line and set the bird free. His wing span was immense.

Whenever we help God's creatures we typically experience different reactions from different people. One morning, before I started to paint a building with some friends, I noticed that a frog had gotten himself caught in a 5 gallon can of paint. He was floating in the paint but because his nose was above the surface he didn't drown. I pulled him out of the paint and started to hose him off. He was very cooperative and it didn't take long. My friends wasted no time in laughing at me for helping the frog. To be sure, the frog wasn't laughing. He had just spent the entire night living with the fear that he was going to die in a vat of paint. The frog and I had something in common that day. Neither one of us could understand the reaction of my friends who laughed at an act of kindness. Maybe I'll see him in Heaven.

I'll share one last experience with you that happened very recently. While running at the beach I noticed a loon being washed up on the shore by the breakers. Every time a wave pushed him under he would surface, shake his head, and was immediately washed under again by another wave. He seemed helpless and unable to swim or fly. I tried to reach into the water to rescue him but the waves kept washing him away from me. Finally I was able to get my hands around him and while carefully folding his wings against his body I lifted him out of the water and walked toward the dry sand. His legs were limp and he seemed completely exhausted. As I walked the last few feet to safety he began to cry like a baby. It was one of the saddest sounds I have ever heard. I sensed that he thought I was going to kill him. I placed him on the sand with one side of his face actually on the sand while the other side was facing the sky. In seconds he closed his eyes and fell asleep. He was breathing heavily but not moving. I was unable to stay with him but inherently knew that he would probably die. I prayed for him.

Wouldn't it be awesome if all the animals and people we have helped during our life time are standing at the gates of Heaven with Jesus, waiting to welcome us? What a home coming that will be!

To my wife Joan
whose patient love has
allowed the child within me
to remain alive and happy.

The Monk
&
The Skunk

Do animals go to Heaven?

John Regan

1

The Secret

Not far from Rome, in the beautiful Italian countryside, an ancient Monastery sits atop a lush green hill basking in the warm summer sunshine. Quietly at first, then with a squeaking sound, a large wooden gate attached to the outside garden slowly opens onto a pathway that leads to the valley below. Suddenly, as if shot from cannon, a habit clad monk comes charging out of the monastery and leaps into the air screaming, YEEEHAAA as he does a flying flip and endless somersaults while hurtling hundreds of feet down the country path to the valley below.

Silently watching from the nearby bushes a stunned skunk audibly utters, "Good grief!! What in the world was that?"

So here is this skunk, stretching his neck out of the bushes, peering down the path into the valley below, searching through the settling dust for whomever or whatever it was that blasted out of the otherwise placid monastery. He sees nothing.

"Well, I'm not going to just sit here" he whispers to himself. "I've got to check this out or Fragrance will never believe me."

Fragrance is his wife and the mother of their two youngsters. Cautiously looking over his shoulder, to make sure there isn't a repeat performance that could potentially run him over, down the path he goes. Halfway to the valley he notices many foot prints and lots of trampled bushes. The trampled bushes, he concludes, are obviously from the summersaults. But, what about the foot prints, and why are there so many? Suddenly he discovers the end coming into view at the very bottom. As he reaches the valley floor a beautiful scene unfolds before him revealing a very large clearing ringed with thick vegetation, hundreds of flowers and a stately oak tree at the far end. And there, sitting under the tree on a large flat boulder was the amazing gymnastic monk. He seemed to be removing a guitar from a case which he had obviously taken from a wooden shed adjacent to the tree. The curious skunk moved quickly through the underbrush, as silently as possibly, in an effort to get closer so he could investigate this unusual monk. The slightest noise would alert the monk who might react in a hostile way causing the skunk to defend himself and spray his attacker. And that was last thing he wanted. Finding a comfortable well hidden spot a few bushes from the clearing, and very close to the monk, he settled down to see what would happen next.

"Ok folks, what would you like to hear" the monk suddenly announced.

Curiously looking around the large clearing the skunk could see no one but the monk. Afraid to stick his head above the tops of the bushes for a more thorough look he decided to just be patient and wait.

"For starters shall we try 'Amazing *Grace' the* monk continued, still addressing a non- existent audience. Immediately the skunk responded by saying **"Sure"** before he panicked and slapped his paw in front of his mouth, realizing he had made a terrible mistake.

Instantly, the monk moved toward the back of the large boulder and searched the clearing for visitors. He saw no one.

Burying himself deeper beneath the underbrush the skunk muttered quietly, "I hope he doesn't see me. I can't go through another attack. I still smell from the last one."

Whispering, the anxious monk began to pray. "Dear lord, I heard a voice, but I don't see anyone. Was it you, or am I just overtired and hearing things"? With that he picked up his guitar and began to sing...
"*Amazing Grace, how sweet the sound,*
That saved a wretch like me....
I once was lost but now am found,
was blind, but now I see."

As the skunk was quietly humming to himself the Monk abruptly stopped. "Wait a minute. Let me try that again in a different key. Ok, here we go again...
"*Amazing Grace, how sweet the sound, that saved a......*

"**Wretch like me**" the skunk forcefully sang... before suddenly realizing he had made a potentially fatal mistake. In a panic, he quickly raced through the underbrush, heading a short distance back up the pathway and settled behind the base of a tall tree.

The Monk was silent, and somewhat fearful. He slowly stood up, placed the guitar back in its case and very quietly returned it to the shed. Frantically trying to think of a way to safely get back to the monastery without being attacked by the owner of the mysterious voice, he suddenly heard the sound of the lunch bell ringing loud and clear from the top of the hill. "YEEEHAAA", he screamed as he leapt from the boulder and raced across the clearing, charging up the hill to safety.

Peering out of the bushes to watch the disappearing Monk, the Skunk sighed with relief and a bit of disappointment. "Gee, it looks like he was more afraid of me than I of him. I sure hope he returns though. That song is my favorite."

The lunch bell rang for the ninth time as the Monk burst through the main door of the Monastery, out of breath and anxious about the mysterious voice in the valley.

"Three more rings until Grace. I guess I can make it to the dining room in time for lunch" he reasoned as he raced down the long stone hallway to the dining room.

"In the name of the Father and of the Son…"
Father Mark the Superior began, just as the Monk rushed into the dining room and sat down next to Father John. As soon as Father Mark finished praying, Father John whispered "Father Charlie, I thought you were having lunch in the valley today."

"John, you won't believe what happened. I was pretending I was playing for an audience and I asked if "Amazing Grace" would be a good choice. Suddenly a voice answered and said 'Sure'. I looked around and didn't see anyone, so I assumed it was my imagination. Moments later I began to sing Amazing Grace, and when I got to the words "wretch like me" that same voice spoke again, and this time it was very loud, and said **'Wretch Like Me'.** I couldn't believe it. I stood on top of the boulder and noticed the bushes between me and the pathway moving as something ran away. I don't know what it was but the voice sounded like a man."

"A man would be too big to run under the bushes like that. Even a kid would be too big Charlie."

"I know John. That's why I freaked out and ran up the hill."

John was very familiar with the hide-a-way Charlie had made for himself in the valley. Clearing the land and planting shrubs and flowers took 2 years of serious back breaking labor. But the result was a beautiful retreat in the valley where the monks could come and listen to Father Charlie sing and play his guitar. It was especially important to Charlie because it offered him a quiet place in nature where he could write new songs and practice singing. This had been his hobby since he entered high school. And now, twenty years later, he had compiled a collection of 42 songs for which he had written both the lyrics and music.

"Charlie... may I speak freely?"

"Sure John."

"Do you think that maybe as you were singing the words, you were also thinking the words, and it was kind of like an echo in your brain'?

"John... I'm not imagining things. I know what I heard. And I heard it twice"

"Well I wouldn't mention it to anyone else."

"Gee thanks. I thought we were friends."

"We are friends Charlie. And I didn't mean I don't believe you. But I'm not sure about the others. There are 27 of us here and you don't want to be explaining yourself every time someone else hears about it."

"Well, I'm going back tomorrow morning, right after Mass. Will you join me and be my witness in case it happens again?"

"I can't. I'm meeting with Tony the roofing contractor in the morning. A few more rains like last week and we could have some major damage if we don't replace at least the main section."

"Ok. I'll go by myself. It probably wouldn't be a good idea to tell anyone else at this point now that you mention it. But if I'm not back by dinner time send a search party. Who knows? There may be a monster down there."

"Relax Charlie. I'll be praying for you"

Father Charles finished lunch and headed to the Chapel. He knew there were real answers for every situation in life and the only person who consistently had those answers was God.

2

Speechless

The rising sun quietly swept across the Italian countryside, gently coming to rest on the Ivy covered walls of the beautiful Monastery. Built in the early 18th century it is home to an order of priests and brothers who spend their lives in a routine of prayer and work. Each monk has a specific job which contributes to the welfare of the others. They also give public retreats on a monthly basis and spend time in between retreats preparing for the next one. One such job is the music ministry which is presided over by Father Charles O'Malley. Born in Ireland, the 34 year old Priest joined the Order after high school and was ordained six years later. Now, happily settled in Italy, Charlie has become very popular among his confreres because of the sing-along concerts he conducts in the monastery and, in recent times, at his outdoor retreat in the valley. Today will be somewhat different however. Today he will attempt to discover who or what the voice in the valley really is. As Holy Mass concluded he headed for the patio garden where the door to the valley was located. True to form, he prepared to open the door, charge to the top of the pathway, leap into the air with a jungle scream, execute an aerial flip, and endless summersaults as he cascaded at top speed to the valley floor below.

"Wait a minute" Charlie reasoned. "If the monster is down there I'll either alert him and scare him off, or, he'll hide and wait to attack me. Maybe I'd better go quietly and surprise him so I can get a good look before he runs away. And if he attacks me I'll probably live because he must be very small to be able to hide under those bushes."

With his plans all set, Charlie opened the door and quietly stepped outside. Slowly and cautiously he descended the hillside stopping every time he heard a twig break or bird moving in the trees. He was so quiet he could hear himself breathing. Half way down the path he suddenly had company. Although he didn't see the eyes peering through the underbrush, they saw him and followed him to the valley floor. As the monk made his way towards the shed to retrieve his guitar, the owner of the eyes raced around the perimeter of the clearing and positioned himself directly behind the boulder Charlie was approaching. There, beneath a flowering Rhododendron bush, the skunk anxiously waited for the music to begin. As Charlie opened his guitar case and began shuffling through his sheet music to see what would interest him today, he noticed his hands slightly trembling.

"Hmmm, I'm more anxious than I expected to be. Let's see... 'How great tho art', 'You are Mine', 'Amazing Grace,'...Whoa, that's the one the mysterious voice approved of. That's it then. This should draw him out of hiding if he's here."

Charlie put the music back in the case, he knew 'Amazing Grace" by heart. Looking around the clearing he slowly put the guitar sling around his shoulder, took a deep nervous breath and began to sing.

*"Amazing Grace, how sweet the sound,
That saved a wretch like me...
I once was lost, but now am found,
was blind, but now, I see."*

As he prepared to sing the next verse he paused, listening hopefully for a response from the mystery voice. Hearing nothing he continued...

*"T'was Grace that taught,
My heart to fear,
And Grace, my fears relieved,
How precious did that Grace appear,
The hour I first believed"*

Still, Charlie heard nothing. While continuing to hum the sounds of Amazing Grace he unconsciously started singing the first verse again.

*"Amazing Grace, how sweet the sound,
That saved a wretch like me..."* Abruptly, he stopped. Holding his breath, his mind raced... "What was that? I heard something, kind of like a sniffle when you have a cold and... there it goes again."

Standing up and removing his guitar Charlie shouted, **"Who is that! Where are you?"**

Silence...

With hands still trembling the anxious priest decided to sing the first verse one more time.

"Amazing......grace.........How...sweet.....the sound............That saved a.....

"Wretch like me".....the voice shouted from the bushes.

Charlie jumped from the rock, ran half way across the clearing, stopped, spun around, ready to dash up the hill if necessary, and screamed... **'Who are you'?**

"Don't worry. I won't hurt you." a quiet voice answered from the bushes behind the boulder.

"I'm not afraid of you" Charlie responded as he inched his way towards the pathway for a quick escape.

The skunk moved quietly through the bushes, attempting to get closer to Charlie while still remaining out of sight. No one spoke. Charlie stood his ground. The skunk remained still.

"Are you a person?" Charlie shouted.

"No, I'm a skunk"; came the quiet answer.

Charlie jumped back, not expecting the response to be so close.

"Skunks can't talk" he insisted.

"Yes they can, the skunk fired back.

"No they can't".

"Yes they can".

"You're not a skunk".

"Yes I am".

"No you're not".

"Yes I am".

Exasperated Charlie ran to the safety of the pathway and screamed... **Prove it!**

"Oh great" the skunk worried... "When he sees how small I am he might throw his guitar at me, or try to hurt me in some other way. I've got a family to worry about. I can't take the chance."

"I can't come out to meet you. I don't trust you. You'll try to hurt me. "

"No I won't"

"Put your guitar down".

Charlie couldn't believe what was happening.

"I'm talking to a skunk and he wants me to put my guitar down so I won't hurt him. This can't be real. I'm losing my mind."

"I'm still waiting".

"Ok. Ok. I'll put my guitar down".

As the anxious monk slowly put his guitar on the ground the bushes slightly moved as the skunk worked his way to the edge of the clearing. Still not visible he made one last appeal. 'Are you sure you won't hurt me?'

"I'm sure" Charlie nervously responded.

Cautiously, the skunk stepped through the bushes into the clearing and held up his two front paws as a sign of peace.

Speechless, Charlie just stood there staring at the skunk. 'This isn't happening' he thought, as his mind raced back and forth between reality and disbelief.

"Ok… let me hear you speak".

Still keeping his distance, the skunk looked at the imposing, 6 foot tall monk and asked; "What's your name?"

"What's my name? You, a skunk, are asking me a real person what my name is. What's **your** name?"

"I asked you first".

"Ok, Ok. You're asking me a human being what my name is and I'm supposed to believe this is really happening and answer you. Well I don't believe this is really happening… I'm sure I must be dreaming."

"You're not dreaming. Trust me. But if you don't have a name, that's all right. I'll just call you 'Friend'."

"No! You don't have to call me 'Friend'. I have a name."

Silence prevailed as the two stared at each other while 20 feet apart. The monk was reluctant to give his name to a demanding skunk, and the skunk was unwilling to be the first to identify himself to a monk. As the wind whispered through the trees Charlie tried not to look at the skunks insistent eyes when he suddenly heard the final words…

"And your name is…?"

"This skunk is too much" Charlie reluctantly admitted to himself. "Ok Mr. Skunk you win. My name is Father Charles O'Malley. My friends call me Charlie. But you can call me Father Charlie."

Unsure if that permission meant he would not be considered a friend the skunk decided to deal with that later. For now it was his turn to identify himself. Standing as tall as possible, and taking a deep breath, he initiated one pronounced step forward and said "Father Charlie, I am pleased to meet you. My name is Aroma".

The incredulous monk quietly whispered…
"Aroma"?

"That is correct. My name is Aroma!"

"Well, Aroma, it is a pleasure meeting you also. I have been wondering where the voice was coming from and now I know. How did you learn to speak?"

"I was born that way".

"Born that way? I didn't think animals could talk, much less be born that way."

"All animals can talk."

"You're kidding".

"No, I'm not kidding. Animals can talk. And they are all born that way."

"Then why can't we hear them speaking?

"They don't speak when you are present because they don't trust you. Humans kill animals."

"True. Humans do kill animals. I don't approve of that, but yes, humans kill animals."

"You don't approve of that? What did you have for breakfast?"

"Bacon and eggs."

"Uh huh", Aroma responded while staring at Father Charlie who awkwardly remained silent while processing this interrogating skunk's line of questioning.

"Well uh…" Charlie began, struggling for an answer he couldn't find.

"That's ok, we'll cover that topic another time", Aroma suggested in an effort to be merciful to his new acquaintance. "I enjoy listening to your music. I have been listening since yesterday when you came charging out of the Monastery and rolled down the hill.'

"Well, that is sort of an exercise for me. It's kind of like running or riding a bicycle. It gets the cob webs out of your system. What is it about my music that you like the most? I noticed that you sang the same words a couple of times. I think they were *"Wretch like me"*.

Aroma was stunned. He hadn't expected that question. It was too soon. He didn't really know Father Charlie. He tried to answer but couldn't find his voice. Charlie sensed something was wrong. Aroma seemed to lose his self assured posture and slowly stepped backward towards the bushes. Speechless himself, Charlie developed an unmistakable look of surprise on his face. Aroma instantly picked up on it and in a moment of panic turned and bolted into the underbrush, running as fast and as far as he could to escape the frightening moment that was paralyzing him. Charlie stood motionless. Trying to absorb the last five minutes, and make sense of it, was proving to be impossible.

"What could I have said that frightened him off like that? Could animals have emotions? I mean he was acting like a human. His fear wasn't to protect his life; it was to protect his personhood. But he's not a person. No one is going to believe this."

Charlie walked to the boulder, placed his guitar in the case and returned it to the shed. Tired and confused he made his way to the path and slowly ascended the hill. "Lord, help me to understand" he prayed as he contemplated the most extraordinary day of his life.

3

Humiliation

Father John sat silently at the head of the table, only occasionally looking at his friend Charlie who hadn't spoken a word since his fellow monks had left the dining room. With his lunch barely touched, Charlie quietly shook his head in dismay. "Why wouldn't they listen to the whole story? I only said a few words and they all began to laugh. You were the only one not laughing at me John. All I said was I met a skunk in the valley today and it actually talked to me. As I was about to relate the experience they all burst into laughter and no one would give me a chance to explain. Even when I held up my hands asking for silence so I could speak, they laughed all the louder."

John was more concerned about Charlie's distress than he was about the rejection of the story. He had never seen his friend sad or heard him complain in the eight years since they had met. And now just a few chairs away his friend was seriously wounded.

"Ignore it Charlie. It's no big deal."

"It is a big deal John. It's a very big deal. And I can't just forget it. That skunk really spoke with me. When I was singing the song 'Amazing Grace' and got to the part 'wretch like me' he sang those words from where he was hiding under the bushes. I also heard what I thought was sniffling, like when someone has a cold. But now that I think about it I have a strong feeling that he was crying. And when we were speaking a little later I mentioned that I heard him sing those words and he became very embarrassed and ran away.

John patiently listened but said nothing. Just an occasional nod and smile was all he contributed to the conversation. He thought it best to let his friend tell his story which 25 of their fellow confreres had refused to hear.

"John, it was such a shock to see this skunk walk out of the bushes and hold up his paws as a gesture of peace and introduce himself. I thought I was dreaming but he assured me I was not."

John was becoming interested although not convinced.

"What did he say?

"He said his name is Aroma"

Struggling to hold back a smile John asked, "The skunk said his name is Aroma?'

"Don't laugh John. I know what you're thinking. Yes, he told me his name is Aroma. But that was only after I told him my name. He had refused to tell me his name until I introduced myself first."

John shifted in his chair and took a deep breath. Before he spoke his mind he wanted Charlie to feel secure in their friendship. He decided to go along for now. "Was there anything else"?

"Yes. He ran from me. Not because I threatened him physically, but because I embarrassed him. And that is not an animal reaction but a human reaction. I don't mean to say that he is human but I think he has a personality, like a person. And he can speak like a person. He told me that all the animals can talk and that they are all born that way. But now I don't know if I will ever see him again."

Obviously perplexed and sad, Charlie just shook his head in silence as he stared at the table. John, although interested, was becoming convinced that Charlie was having some sort of emotional problem. But, friends are friends and John remembered the slogan 'a friend in need is a friend indeed'.

"Charlie, how about the two of us go to the valley in the morning to see if we can figure this out? There must be an answer."

Charlie's face lit up like the sunrise. "Wow John! That's a perfect idea. I can start to sing and hopefully Aroma will hear me and return to the clearing. And you can bring the video camera and film the meeting from a distance." John nodded in agreement but realized he would have to smuggle the Video Camera out of the monastery. If anyone noticed him bringing it to the valley they would become suspicious and think that he had believed Charlie and was going to film talking skunks. And John was not ready to deal with that scenario.

"Sure Charlie. I'll get it from the office today so we'll have it ready to go in the morning. Does 8:30, right after Mass sound good to you?"

"Yep, I'll be ready. Thanks for believing in me John"

John didn't respond. He politely smiled and left the dining room.

4

Reality

Charlie was waiting for John at the patio garden gate. They had left Mass together but John needed to retrieve the video camera. Impatient to get down to the valley Charlie pushed open the old wooden gate and walked to the top of the pathway. Gazing at the vegetation and the path that wound its way down to the hide-a-way he worried about his relationship with his fellow monks. "Gee, if we don't see and film Aroma today it's a sure thing that John and everyone else will think I'm crazy. I know Aroma is real and I know he can talk but without proof my reputation is ruined."

"Let's go Charlie" John announced as he surprised Charlie out of his daydream and walked up beside him.

"Oh, hi John, I was just thinking about Aroma and hoping we can get him to talk on camera so I won't be the laughing stock of the monastery."

"That might be more of a challenge than you think Charlie. I wouldn't expect too much from an animal."

John was doing everything he could to keep his brother priest and friend peaceful. He sensed that he wasn't living in reality and, for whatever reason, was living in a fantasy world.

"Well, he is an animal, yes, but don't convince yourself that he is dumb because of that. He can talk John, and he will if we're able to demonstrate that we are safe and don't intend to hurt him."

THE MONK & THE SKUNK

John didn't have the heart to tell Charlie what he was really thinking, but he inherently believed that Charlie was mistaken and suffering from some sort of mental fatigue. But, for now, he intended to go along while secretly hoping the skunk would not show up and the whole matter would slowly fade away.

"Let's go John. I'll lead the way. Be very quiet and try not to step on any twigs that will snap and warn him that we're coming. I want it to be a surprise. When we reach the valley I'll get my guitar from the shed and start playing the song he likes and we'll probably see him suddenly appear."

John whispered "ok" and off they went with Charlie leading the way. Suddenly Charlie spotted animal tracks in the dirt path and pointed them out to John. John nodded and picked his video camera up to his eyes and started filming the tracks and the path that led to the valley floor. Slowly they descended the winding trail until they reached the hide-a-way. While John filmed the beautiful scenery Charlie anxiously rushed to the shed to retrieve his guitar. As John slowly walked around the perimeter of the clearing, filming as he went, Charlie removed his guitar from the case and stood on top of the flat boulder and started to play *Amazing Grace*. When John reached the shed he aimed his camera at Charlie and recorded his efforts to bring Aroma out into the open. Charlie sang the first few lines over and over again, stopping at the part where Aroma would blurt out "wretch like me" but no sound was heard from the valley.

"Maybe a different song will work Charlie. You've played that one five times."

"I know John but it worked before and it should work now. Maybe he left the valley permanently. He was very embarrassed yesterday."

"Animals don't get embarrassed Charlie. He was probably frightened."

Charlie was becoming impatient, he knew the truth but no one would believe him.

"John, I made every effort to gain his trust. I didn't frighten him. Trust me... he definitely was embarrassed."

"Well, let's go into the woods a bit and look for him" John suggested.

Charlie jumped down from the boulder and headed into the woods playing *Amazing Grace* as he went. With John right behind, camera in hand and filming, they both began to sing in an unusually loud tone. Occasionally birds in the trees above would fly away, obviously frightened by the parade of monks singing and marching through their back yard. As he continued singing Charlie desperately hoped Aroma would appear because he was certain that after another twenty minutes or so John would lose heart and declare the mission a failure.

"Charlie, why don't we circle back and try around the clearing again; it's been ten minutes since you started singing and the only life I've seen is a few birds."

Charlie's heart sank. John was his best friend and now even he was starting to abandon him.

"Ok John. I'll go around the clearing a few more times. That will probably work"

As they completed the third lap of the perimeter

THE MONK & THE SKUNK

Charlie stopped by the boulder. Silent, eyes desperately searching the clearing and surrounding valley, he slowly put his guitar down on the boulder and sighed... "I don't know what to say John. This is the most discouraging moment of my life. I know the truth and you don't. And even though we are friends it wouldn't be fair of me to ask you to believe me any longer. Aroma is real. He can talk, he did talk, and he probably will talk again. But you don't know that and I can't expect you to defend me when you have no evidence that I'm telling the truth. In fact you probably think I'm going crazy."

"Charlie, my friend, I don't think you're going crazy, but I do think you might need a vacation so you can get away and rest."

Charlie slowly began to put his guitar into its case and walked it to the shed. As he turned to walk back towards John he looked at the ground and hoping John wouldn't see, wiped a tear from his eye. John noticed but looked the other way. Annoyed by the situation and feeling powerless to help his friend, John suddenly jumped on top of the boulder and screamed into the woods. **"Aroma!! If you really exist and you really can talk then come and help Father Charlie. He's been making a fool of himself for you. No one believes him. They laugh at him."**

Charlie felt guilty that his friend had to do what he probably regarded as insanity. But John was that kind of person. He was a friend.

"Thanks John", Charlie whispered as he struggled to speak beyond his emotions. "Aroma will probably show up some other time.

John realized he needed to bring Charlie back to reality; and doing silly things like yelling into the woods for a fictitious skunk wasn't helping.

"Charlie, I think I need to be more realistic if I really want to help you. I don't believe there is a skunk, much less one that can talk. I think you need to forget about this and spend some time in prayer. Let's head back and make it in time for lunch."

Charlie was crushed. Even John no longer believed him. "John, I'm sorry you don't believe me and I'm sorry you had to go through this. I'm going to stay here for a while. Maybe Aroma will return."

"Charlie you're making a mistake".

John turned and headed toward the pathway and just as he was about to ascend the hill a loud voice bellowed…..**STOP!!** Spinning around John was stunned to see a small skunk standing at the edge of the clearing 10 feet away.

"Aroma! Aroma, you came back" Charlie cried in relief as he rushed to greet him.

Aroma dashed to the other side of the clearing thinking Charlie was going to hurt him.

"No! No! Don't worry Aroma I won't hurt you. I was just going to welcome you."

"Father Charlie you can't charge at me like that. I'm an animal and we instinctively run for protection."

"Oh, I'm sorry Aroma."

Aroma stepped closer… "Father Charlie"…

"Just call me Charlie Aroma. You don't have to call me Father. Just call me Charlie. It's ok. Really"!

"Well I wasn't sure after that bizarre instruction you gave me yesterday, 'My friends call me Charlie but you can call me Father Charlie'. It sounded like I was second class or something."

John was speechless, stunned into silence by this incredible exchange between a talking skunk and his brother priest. Not only was this mysterious skunk speaking, just as Charlie had insisted, but he also was a sarcastic intellect.

"That was just a formal suggestion Aroma. We had just met and really didn't know each other that well. But please, call me Charlie from now on."

"I heard you call this man Father John. Is he safe to be around? Many humans are dangerous?"

"Yes. He is very safe; right John"?

John nodded.

"Can't he speak"? Aroma quipped.

"Yes I can speak. I'm just in a bit of shock. I'm not sure if I will wake up in the morning and this will all have been a dream. And yes, I am safe."

"John brought a video camera to film some of our conversations so our brother monks will believe me. So far they don't believe that you can talk Aroma and they probably think I am crazy."

"That will not be a good Idea Charlie. I prefer that you do not video tape me because, if you do, there will be hundreds of people coming to the valley to see me. And then you and I will not be able to converse."

An obvious look of relief came over Charlie's face. He hadn't anticipated Aroma's eagerness to speak with him.

"Do you mean you would like to speak with me Aroma?"

"Yes I would. But it is confidential and Father

John would not be permitted to listen and you would not be allowed to share our conversations with him or anyone else."

"That's fine Aroma" Charlie offered.

"Would you prefer I leave" John suggested.

"I'm not ready today", Aroma replied. It will have to be another day. This is too important. I need time to prepare."

"How will I know when you're ready", Charlie asked.

"You come here every day Charlie. When I'm ready I'll contact you. It was nice meeting you Father John."

As Aroma returned to the woods, John and Charlie just stared at each other in complete silence. Both realized that not a word of their experience would be believed by anyone, especially their fellow monks. They were having trouble believing it themselves. As they trudged up the hill John warned against sharing the day's events with their religious community. Charlie readily agreed.

"At least you know the truth John. I was afraid you would never believe me and write me off as a lunatic."

"I didn't believe you before today Charlie, but I do now. I just wish there was some way we could share this with our brothers. But, for now, we'll just have to be patient and wait to see what Aroma has to say about that."

5

Trapped

Charlie stared at the ceiling as he struggled to greet the new day. The sun was just beginning to clear the horizon, and the birds were responding with their usual song of joy.

"Wow, 6:30, and I slept straight thru the night. Nine hours, that's unusual" he thought as he sat up and reflected on yesterdays encounter with Aroma. "I'd better get down to the valley as soon as possible. Aroma wants to talk and I don't want to forget anything about our conversation so I'll bring a notepad and pen. I can't believe this is happening".

Charlie was a structured person. Everything had a time and place and everything needed to be categorized and in order. For Charlie it made life easier and more productive. He was a doer, and his friends knew they could rely on him to deliver whatever he promised. Heading down the main hallway to the dining room he spotted John walking through the doors, followed by several monks including the superior, Father Mark.

"Gee, I hope John sits by himself. I really need to speak with him privately."

As soon as Charlie entered the dining room Father Mark welcomed him with a smile.

"Father Charles, I haven't heard anything further about your adventures in the valley."

"Oh, good morning Father Mark, I uh…I didn't think it was appropriate to discuss that topic any longer, I uh…"

Father Mark smiled as he broadcast a loud friendly laugh across the dining room and patted Charlie on the back. "We all have humorous imaginings from time to time Father Charles. Your brother Friars understand. We'll just put that in the back of the history book and forget about it. Ha! Ha!"

Charlie struggled to smile as Father Mark walked to the head of the dining room and sat down. As he looked for a seat he noticed John waving to him from the corner table. He immediately joined him and took his seat just as Father Mark stood to say Grace. As the final 'Amen' echoed across the room John passed the oatmeal to Charlie. "What did Father Mark say to you?"

"He excused me for my imaginings and put the issue to rest. He was cordial and friendly but obviously telling me to forget it."

"What did you say?"

"Nothing."

"We better keep this between the two of us Charlie, ... at least for now."

"I agree John. In the mean time I'd better get down there today. I think Aroma has some kind of a problem"

John stared into space. "I still can't believe this. It's unreal. How could a skunk talk? Skunks can't talk! They just plain can't talk!"

6

Wretch like me.

Charlie stood pensively at the Garden Gate, unable to bring himself to perform his usual flying flip routine. His mental fatigue had drained him and left him uncertain as to how he should behave in this next encounter with Aroma.

"I guess I'll just walk down the path in a normal way. Not quietly, because I want Aroma to know I'm on the way, but not blasting out of the gate and flying into the air either. Aroma will think I'm nuts and he wants to have a serious conversation."

So down the path Charlie went, feeling awkward and out of sync with his real self, which is usually full of life and optimism about the future. As he passed all the familiar twists and turns his mind raced back to his previous entries into the valley during the past few years, and, suddenly, he stopped in his tracks.

"Hold the phone. Aroma approached me because he felt comfortable with me... the real me. But now I'm acting in a way that I think he would prefer, which is illogical. I should just be me...the real me."

Charlie spun around, doing a complete about face, and charged back up the hill. Out of breath, but determined to be himself, he raced into the garden, repositioned himself for a classic grand entry into the valley and blasted out through the gate, running at full speed to the top of the path and flew into the air screaming YeeHaaaa, as he excitedly performed an Olympic flip and careened down the hill with endless summersaults. Landing on his feet amidst a cloud of dust on the valley floor he felt as though he had been reborn.

"Wow!! I needed that" he yelled into the clearing as he dusted himself off.

"Glad you could make it Charlie" a voice announced from the opposite side of the clearing.

Stunned, Charlie scanned the clearing to see who the owner of the voice was. Anxious, and impatient, his eyes raced around the perimeter stopping suddenly at the boulder under the big tree. There, as big as day, sitting on top of the boulder while leaning against the tree, was a small, black and white skunk.

"Aroma, you're here".

"Yes, I'm here Charlie, and I trust you came alone as I requested."

"I have Aroma. No one is with me and to my knowledge no one else will be coming to the valley today."

"Good! I would like to speak with you. Is this a good place to sit?"

"Yes, you're fine right where you are. May I sit next to you?"

"You may, but before you do I would like you to give me your word that you won't hurt me."

"I give you my word Aroma. You can trust me."

Charlie was in mild shock and unable to quiet his racing mind. This was happening much faster than he had imagined. He felt unprepared. As he approached the boulder he remembered Father John saying that he would be praying for this potential event.

"Prayer, that's the answer" Charlie decided as he stepped onto the rock in silence. He knew that the slightest wrong move would send Aroma racing into the woods.

"Well, good morning Aroma" Charlie nervously offered as he slowly sat down 8 feet from Aroma.

"Good morning Charlie. I hope you have at least an hour to chat?"

"Yes, I do Aroma."

Charlie was incredulous and almost disbelieving as he stared at Aroma who appeared to be no bigger than a small dog.

"Aroma, before we begin, would it be alright with you if I said a prayer?"

"Sure, that's fine with me. But I need to tell you that we animals don't know any prayers, and we are unsure of the concept of God. We are aware that you have many prayers, and we have heard quite a few of them. So I won't be praying with you, however, I will be listening."

"I understand," Charlie responded and said, "Now I will pray. Dear God our Father, Aroma and I will be having a conversation. He is an animal, and I am a human. Please help us to understand one another. This is a new experience for both of us. Please tell us what to think and what to say. Thank you for this wonderful opportunity. We pray to you through the loving heart of your son Jesus. Amen."

Charlie looked at Aroma who seemed to be in deep thought. Suddenly, as if he sensed Charlie's glance, Aroma looked in Charlie's direction and said "Amen". Unsure of the next move Charlie decided to ask Aroma what he would like to discuss.

"Aroma, I'm all ears and have plenty of time. You

said you would like to chat."

"Uh, yes... yes that's right Charlie. I would like to chat."

Suddenly Aroma seemed self conscious and hesitant. Charlie was determined to not say the wrong thing and send Aroma into a panic, so he decided to say nothing.

After a few seconds of uncomfortable silence, Aroma sat up from his relaxed position, looked away, and said "Charlie, I have a problem".

Patiently waiting for an explanation which, after ten seconds, never materialized, Charlie offered a quiet "ok".

Aroma shifted in his sitting position again and seemed to be having difficulty beginning.

"Well, what type of problem do you have" Charlie asked, barely above a whisper. He was trying to be sensitive to Aroma's obvious fear or embarrassment or both.

Aroma leaned back against the tree, as if he were searching for a more secure position, looked up at the sky and said, "Charlie ... I feel guilty. And I can't get rid of it."

"What do you feel guilty about?"

"Many things; I have been feeling this way for months. And, as time goes by, the list keeps growing. I even wake up in the middle of the night and worry about this guilty feeling."

Charlie was amazed. An animal is telling him he feels guilty. Charlie believes animals don't have souls and if they don't have souls then how could they experience guilt.

"Would you like to give me an example of your guilt feelings?"

Eager to lift the burden on his conscience Aroma instantly responded, "I'll give you an example Charlie but you must promise me that you'll keep this between us."

"I give you my word Aroma. I won't tell another soul."

Aroma scanned the clearing to make sure no other animals or humans were near. Leaning forward towards Charlie he whispered, "I sprayed a friend of mine on purpose. I just meant it as a joke but he hasn't spoken to me or forgiven me since. I've never done anything like that before. When I was a youngster my father taught me to always spray a predator from an upwind position so the spray doesn't fall back on me. Well, I sprayed Waldo from a downwind position and the spray went all over both of us. I was in such a mischievous mood that I didn't think about what I was doing. When I arrived home my wife and two sons were furious with me. I smelled for weeks. In addition, I have heard from other animals that Waldo had the same problem with his family when he went home. Waldo usually comes to visit me once every week or two but I haven't seen or heard from him in over a month. Because of that I concluded that he probably hasn't forgiven me. And that only compounds my sense of guilt. Do you know what I mean Charlie?"

"Well, uh, yes Aroma. Yes, I do understand."

Charlie was experienced hearing confessions from humans and usually had sound advice for the penitent. But hearing an animal proclaiming his guilt, and seeking advice, was so unusual that Charlie found himself somewhat speechless.

"Uh, well, let's see… have you considered speaking with him and apologizing and asking for forgiveness."

"I did apologize immediately after I sprayed him. And before he went home I asked him to forgive me, but he just stormed off instead."

"That was more than a month ago. Have you considered going to visit him and apologizing again and asking for forgiveness?"

"Yes, but he is much bigger than I. And if he gets mad I could be risking my life."

"How much bigger could he possibly be? I thought most skunks are about the same size."

"He's not a skunk Charlie."

"He's not a skunk? Oh, I thought he was a skunk. So what kind of animal is he?

"Waldo is a wild boar".

Charlie was trying to keep a straight face and not laugh for fear he would offend Aroma. Attempting to visualize the scene of a huge wild boar and a small skunk having sociable conversations amused him. "Ok…Waldo is a wild boar, and you're a skunk, and you're friends. I think it is worth the risk of him getting mad. Your friendship is more important than a few frowns from Waldo."

"If he gets mad Charlie it will be more than just a few frowns. He's a wild boar, about 400 pounds, and I'm a skunk, about 10 pounds. I don't know if you've ever seen a charging wild boar, but let me assure you, it's not a pretty picture."

Charlie had to think fast, there didn't seem to be a ready solution.

"Aroma, how about a meeting with a referee present; someone to help with the moments of contention? If you like, I will offer to be the referee at your meeting, just to keep the peace, so you can proceed in a constructive manner and bring healing to your friendship."

Aroma's face lit up with a big smile. "Gee! That's a great idea Charlie."

Charlie was elated. This was the first time he had seen Aroma smile. "Wonderful, I think we have the answer now Aroma. Just let me know when you and Waldo will be available and I'll make a point of reserving the time."

Aroma stood and jumped to the ground. "Thanks Charlie. I'll try to contact Waldo." As he ran to the edge of the clearing he turned and with a brand new smile assured Charlie... "I'll keep you posted."

7

Diplomacy

Aroma was awake before sunrise. His imminent search for Waldo had increased his anxiety level to the point of near panic. Sleep had become almost impossible as his mind raced through the endless possibilities of danger. Venturing into wild boar country was something most skunks and smaller animals would never attempt. Although wild boars usually consumed plants for their diet, they also consumed small animals. Waldo had mentioned that danger to Aroma during one of their many meetings. And while Waldo was strictly a vegetarian he nevertheless warned Aroma to be wary of other wild boars that lived in his neighborhood. 'Keep a constant eye on them my friend. They may look nonchalant as they graze the field grass but they're just waiting for you to take your eyes off of them; and in a flash, before you know it, they're on top of you at full speed. And that good buddy is 40 miles per hour.' Aroma recalled all of this as he finished his vegetarian breakfast. Like Waldo he thought eating other animals was cruel and unnecessary. Waldo's warning was an important consideration for Aroma as he prepared to venture into wild boar country. Should he be attacked he could scream for help and hope that Waldo would be in the vicinity and rush to his rescue. Waldo was much larger than many of the other boars that Aroma had seen in Waldo's neighborhood. And it just stood to reason that he would have some influence on the other animals. Typically, Waldo would travel to

THE MONK & THE SKUNK

Aroma's neighborhood to pay a visit but occasionally Aroma would visit Waldo and it always made him nervous. Today was one of those days, but Aroma was determined to make the trip just the same. He could no longer live with the sense of guilt that had burdened him for the past several months and this seemed to be the only remedy. To make peace with his longtime friend was the goal and Aroma was resolved to finding him... today!

"Aroma, you're up very early. Didn't you sleep well?"

Surprised to hear his wife's voice Aroma turned to see her and their youngsters emerging from the entrance to their home. They lived in a spacious hollow at the base of a very large oak tree.

"Fragrance honey, I hope I didn't wake you. I'm about to begin my search for Waldo. I'll be leaving in a few minutes."

"No, you didn't wake us. We didn't sleep very well, we heard you tossing all night. We just came out to say goodbye."

Aroma had made a point of saying goodbye to his family the night before, but apparently for them it wasn't enough. They loved him dearly and were concerned for his safety. They knew that he and Waldo were at odds and they were doubtful about Waldo's loyalty should Aroma be attacked.

"Gee, I'm sorry I kept you awake honey. I couldn't sleep knowing I would be looking for Waldo in his territory which, as you know, can be dangerous. And because we haven't seen each other since our falling out, I'm not sure he will come to help me if I get in trouble."

"I was thinking the same thing. Maybe it would be better if you waited for Waldo to visit you again and then you could reconcile with one another".

"I doubt Waldo will ever visit again. He was really mad".

Fragrance looked directly at Aroma with devoted concern in her eyes. Aroma recognized her silent expression and was deeply touched. He returned the glance and she instantly understood. This was a private transmittal of love from one to the other that had developed after many years.

"Don't worry" Aroma assured her, "I'll be back before sundown tomorrow."

As the sun inched closer to the edge of night Aroma gave everyone a final hug and began the journey to find Waldo. Moving in an easterly direction he could see long shadows beginning to appear in front of the trees as the sun slowly filled the sky with light. His first concern was crossing the river which separated the valley from the grassy plains to the east. Usually the rocks he needed for stepping stones were dry and above the water level at this time of year. But during the spring thaw flooding usually covered the rocks and crossing would be impossible. As he approached the river bank he was delighted to find the water level to be lower than anticipated and many places were available for a safe crossing. Although Aroma knew very well that other dangers existed he accepted them as part of life in the wild. Unlike humans who had safe houses and police to call in case of danger, animals live in constant fear of one another. They have no one to turn to for help. Aroma was aware of the human expression 'survival of the fittest' which, to him, meant that bigger animals kill smaller animals. But he just couldn't understand why it had to be that way. As he emerged from the shadows of the tall trees lining the river bank he cautiously searched the opposite side looking for any danger. Confident that there were no predators waiting for him he turned his attention to the river itself. Occasionally he had seen bear fishing and he knew that he would be a prime target for a hungry bear. Seeing nothing, he decided it was time to cross. The river was about 150 feet wide and as Aroma began to cross he became increasingly concerned about falling into the water. Although he could swim, the current was strong enough to take him down stream and he didn't know what to expect on the opposite side further down the river. About mid stream the rocks became smaller and he slowed his pace, carefully stepping from one to the next. Suddenly the sun seemed to go behind a cloud although he remembered the sky had been clear. Stopping temporarily, he looked heavenward and was shocked to see an extremely large eagle circling above. Terrified, he began to race across the rocks knowing the eagle could dive and be upon him in seconds. With only 50 feet remaining to safety he panicked to see the Eagle in a full dive with wings almost closed racing directly toward him. Desperate to avoid certain death he jumped over several rocks at a time risking a fall into the river. Just as he made a giant leap for a large flat rock twenty feet from shore he saw the eagle's razor sharp talons about to grab him. Petrified he dove into the water as searing pain raced through his body from the eagles talons digging into his skull and tearing down his back all the way to his tail. Barely escaping death He still had to swim to shore while the eagle circled above waiting to strike again. Desperately fighting the current Aroma noticed blood in the water as he reached for a rock to pull himself up upon. As he sat on the rock trying to catch his breath the eagle dove again. Immediately Aroma jumped back into the river pushing himself below the surface while holding onto the rock. The eagle swooped back up into the sky. Climbing back onto the rock Aroma dashed across the remaining rocks and jumped onto the river bank. Racing towards the trees he could see the eagle diving again. Just as he reached the first tree he threw himself behind the trunk as the eagle flashed by, inches from his face, and soared heavenward once again. Running further into the woods he felt safe enough to stop and inspect his wounds. Most of the bleeding had stopped. The cold river water had helped and now he would have to slow down in order to prevent further bleeding. Wet, and still trembling from his ordeal, Aroma replayed the last few minutes in his mind.

"Why do eagles and bears have to kill? It doesn't make sense. I eat plants and fruits and vegetables. I'm healthy and strong. Maybe they're just too lazy to find food because killing is the easy way. I can't understand it."

As he settled back to rest Aroma sensed an obligation to thank the God that Charlie knew. But he wasn't sure if there really was a God. And even if there was a God he didn't know how to express his thanks. So for now he would just rest. Exhaustion from his ordeal had sapped his strength and he needed time to recuperate.

8

Dilemma

John waited a few minutes after prayer for Charlie to arrive but his scrambled eggs were getting cold so he decided to begin without him. "Kind of unusual for Charlie not to show up for breakfast" he pondered, although Charlie had complained at dinner the night before that he sensed a cold coming on. As John finished his breakfast his mind recalled their meeting with Aroma. 'First I didn't believe that Aroma existed, and even less that he could talk. Although I witnessed that tiny skunk actually speaking directly to me, I still can't believe it.'

John was aware of the meeting Charlie had with Aroma but he knew nothing of the content of their conversation. And according to Aroma's instructions Charlie did not have permission to reveal anything to anyone. Finishing his breakfast and concerned about Charlie's absence he decided to head to Charlie's room to see if he had overslept. As he turned down the last corridor to the living quarters he could see Father Mark knocking on Charlie's door.

"Good morning Father Mark. It appears we both had the same concern for Father Charles. "

"Yes... good morning Father John. I missed Father Charles at breakfast so I'm making sure he is all right. Father Charles, it is Father Mark. Are you all right?"

Silence!

Knock! Knock! "Father Charles it is Father Mark. May I open the door?"

The silence continued as Father Mark and John

exchanged concerned glances.

"Father Charles I am going to open the door".

As Father Mark opened the door he slowly entered the darkened room and turned on the light. Moving from the light switch he was shocked to see Charlie lying in bed staring at the ceiling, in a complete sweat, and trying unsuccessfully to move or speak. Instantly he moved to his side and put his hand on Charlie's forehead. "He's burning up Father John. Get some of the priests to help us. We must get him to the hospital immediately."

John ran through the monastery, pleading with everyone he met to come to the aid of Charlie. Racing back to the room he was followed by 6 monks who were praying out loud as they ran down the hallway. Father Mark had already sat Charlie up in his bed and was attempting to help him stand when help arrived at the door.

"We can carry him Father Mark, he's much too weak to walk" John offered as everyone piled into the room. "Just let him lay on the mattress and we'll carry him to the bus."

Moments later eight Monks raced down the long hallway of the ancient Monastery with Charlie on his mattress covered with two blankets and trembling. As they reached the courtyard where the bus was usually parked, another Monk had already started the engine and moved it to the front entrance.

"Keep him on the mattress and we'll put him in the aisle between the seats" Father Mark ordered. In mere seconds nine Monks and their very sick confrere were barreling down the hillside to the main highway which led to Rome. The hospital was 9 miles away, and it appeared that every minute would count.

"I think he must have galloping pneumonia my brother Priests" Father Mark somberly announced. I've seen this before and he has all of the symptoms."

John began to lead his fellow priests in prayer. His concern for his friend caused him to completely forget about Aroma and his need for Charlie's help. With his eyes riveted on Charlie, his prayer became very intense as he pleaded with God to spare his life. As the bus rounded the last turn before the straight run to Mercy Hospital, Father Mark anointed Charlie with Chrism oil. Moments later, as they pulled into the emergency entrance, Father John jumped out and ran inside to alert the medical staff. In less than 2 minutes Charlie was being loaded onto a stretcher while the doctor in charge discussed with Father Mark the treatment Charlie would receive. Noting that his age and physical condition was in his favor, the doctor was optimistic about the outcome. Once Charlie was admitted to intensive care the monks gathered in the waiting room. After a few minutes of discussion they decided to take turns keeping vigil and communicating updates to the Monastery. For now, the only option was to pray and be patient.

9

Reluctant Loyalty

Reaching the top of the last hill which separates the valley from the high plains, Aroma scanned the distant horizon looking for any sign of wild boars. This was the fringe of their habitat and from here to Waldo's neighborhood, about 2 miles, Aroma needed to use extreme caution. Waldo had warned him time and again that most boars looking for animals to eat would patrol the perimeters of their territory hoping to catch victims that had unknowingly wandered into their stomping grounds.

Still suffering pain from the eagles attack Aroma was grateful that the bleeding had completely stopped. "As long as I'm not attacked again my wounds should heal in a few days. The main challenge for now is to get across these grassy fields without one of Waldo's friends killing me."

Slowly descending the hill, the grass became taller as Aroma progressed onto the plains. About a half mile later he had to frequently stand on his hind paws to see above the prairie grass which was now about two feet high. From past experiences he knew that there was a clearing a short distance ahead which would make it much easier for him to spot trouble. Unfortunately it would also make it easier for his predators to spot him. And with the clearing being a quarter of a mile across he would have to run at top speed to reach the other side safely. The slightest delay could expose him to life threatening danger. As he reached the edge of the clearing his mind shifted into high gear. "This is the place I dread the most. Every time I cross the clearing I see a boar, but so far none have ever seen me. If I run at top speed I need about two minutes to make it to the other side. But that is tough to maintain and I usually have to stop for a 15 second rest."

After scanning the perimeter on both sides, and detecting no animals, he concluded it was as safe as could be expected and decided to make his move. Taking a deep breath Aroma bolted out of the tall grass and began to race toward the other side. Trying to keep his heavy breathing as quiet as possible the only other sound was the pattering of his paws on the ground.

"Fifteen seconds and no animals yet" he whispered. "If I keep up this pace I'll have to rest half way across."

Frantically looking in all directions, including the sky, he detected no danger and continued pushing himself for another forty five seconds. Exhausted and out of breath as he reached the middle of the clearing he slowly stopped and moved as close to the ground as possible.

"If I stay low I probably won't be seen" he hoped as he regained his strength for the last half of the treacherous crossing. "Twenty seconds is all I can risk and then I have to move. This is too dangerous".

Taking one last look at the safety of the tall grass on the other side of the clearing he spotted no danger. As he quickly looked back at the side he just left Aroma was stunned to see two boars slowly walking out of the grass and in his direction. He assumed the larger one was a male and the smaller of the two a female.

"No! I don't believe this. It will take me a minute to get to the other side. They can catch me in less than 30 seconds."

Aroma was in a near panic. He decided to risk a few precious seconds to see if they would change direction and he could wait them out. In his mind he quietly prayed... "God, if you are real please help me". Suddenly the boars began to wander along the edge of the grass while staying in the clearing. As they moved further and further away from his position his panic gave way to logic and he resolved to stay put until they were far enough away for him to make his final run safely.

"That's it. Keep going. Keep going. I can wait. Just another minute or so and you'll be far enough away so I can make it to the grass."

Aroma's wishful thinking was suddenly sabotaged when the two boars once again turned in his direction and moved closer with every step. Realizing that waiting was no longer an option, Aroma made a split second decision he knew might cost him his life, and he charged for the tall grass on the other side of the clearing. Seconds later one of the boars spotted him and began to run in his direction. He could see it was the smaller one and hoped it was slower than the larger boar which, so far, was still walking. Half way to the grass Aroma was terrified to see that he wasn't going to make it. The charging boar was closing too fast. In a desperate effort to save his life he screamed "WALDO!! SAVE ME!!" As the boar closed in Aroma could feel the ground shaking under the weight of its pounding hoofs and hear the snorting of its heavy breath. Suddenly the ground began to tremble even more as the larger boar joined the race and was catching up to the smaller one. Seconds later the larger boar let out a load squealing noise as it passed the smaller boar and closed in on Aroma. Racing to save his life Aroma inherently knew it was too late. He knew he was doomed. Pounding hoofs, snorting and hot breath were upon him as he felt large teeth surround his back and bite down. Convinced death was imminent he held his breath and closed his eyes. Gradually the boar stopped running and began to walk toward a tree. Aroma couldn't move but could see that the other boar was walking away. He assumed he would be killed shortly. As his executioner reached the tree he lifted Aroma to a low lying branch and released him. Shaking in his bones Aroma didn't move not knowing what to do. As he looked at the boar who was still snorting, and out of breath, Aroma suddenly burst into tears. Struggling to speak he blurted out…"WALDO! Waldo you saved me. You saved me Waldo. I thought I was going to die."

Waldo said nothing. He just stared at Aroma.

Trembling and still sobbing Aroma pleaded, "I came out here to find you Waldo. I wanted to see if we could talk things over. I met a human who is a Monk, and he has agreed to counsel with us; to help us be friends again."

As Aroma continued speaking, Waldo listened, but refused to respond.

10

Now What?

Three critical days had passed and Charlie was moved from intensive care to a room on the second floor. One by one his brother priests would visit with him spending only short amounts of time as his strength had been depleted from the pneumonia. John was the first to arrive each day and today he spoke with the head nurse before entering Charlie's room.

"He is improving steadily Father John. We anticipate discharging him in a week or so if all goes well. His delirium from the high fever has ceased and he is now speaking in a logical and coherent manner. How is his friend Aroma doing? He spoke frequently about his concern for him when he was delirious in intensive care. I asked Father Mark but he didn't seem to know Aroma."

John was shocked to hear the nurse speak of Aroma. "Oh, uh I imagine Aroma is okay. I will check when I get back to the Monastery. I'm happy to hear Father Charlie is doing much better. Thank you."

As John walked into Charlie's room he was encouraged to see him sitting up in bed and smiling. "Hi Charlie, you look great. How do you feel?"

"John thanks for visiting. I feel strong enough to go home but they won't release me for at least a week I'm told.

"Charlie, I have to tell you this quickly before anyone else shows up to visit. The nurse just told me that you were speaking about Aroma when you were delirious in intensive care. She later asked Father Mark how Aroma was doing and he said he didn't know Aroma."

"Oh No! I hope he has forgotten about that. I don't want to discuss it with him. He'll probably think I'm insane. In the meantime I'm expecting Aroma to show up and I will need to meet with him. I can't tell you why because of our agreement to keep our discussions secret, but I do need to be available to him at any moment. I don't want him to think I've abandoned him and reneged on my commitment to be available."

"I could meet with him Charlie but he has already said that I could not be present during your discussions."

"I remember John, but under the circumstances we need at least to keep him informed so he doesn't lose heart. Maybe you could go to the valley and call him saying you have an important message from Father Charlie. He might answer you."

"I'll give it a try Charlie. I'll go first thing in the morning. In the meantime you better pray about this. I don't think Aroma is going to trust me."

11

Negotiations

Waldo's silence was making Aroma's efforts toward healing their friendship very difficult. Five minutes had passed, and while Waldo would listen to Aroma's explanations and requests to meet with Father Charlie, he would not respond. He appeared to be uninterested and would make very little eye contact. Aroma was still shaking from his terrifying experience and realized that the smaller boar could have caught and killed him had Waldo not intervened.

"Thank you for saving my life Waldo. I could have easily been killed. I knew there was great danger in my coming to your neighborhood but I wanted to make peace between the two of us. What I did to you was inexcusable, but, as I have already mentioned, it was only meant to be a joke. I was just kidding."

Waldo remained silent as he stared into the distance with a look of impatience on his face.

"And I did apologize to you Waldo, several times. I hope you will forgive me."

Waldo's silence continued.

"Aren't you going to speak Waldo? Don't you have anything to say?"

Suddenly Waldo's demeanor changed as a look of anger replaced his impatience.

"Do I have anything to say? Of course I have something to say, Aroma! I have plenty to say! But why should I say anything at all to someone who was supposed to be my best friend, and out of the blue, with no warning at all, sprays me with that horrible smelling stuff?"

"I'm sorry Waldo. I should not have done that. But I did apologize, several times, and ...

"Apologize? Do you think an apology can wipe away an outrageous uncalled for attack? You, my best friend, without any provocation what so ever, attack me in the same manner as you would a predator. You've got to be kidding Aroma. An apology just doesn't cut it."

Aroma was trying to absorb everything Waldo had just said including the absence of any forgiveness. As he stared at his angry friend, he quietly thought, 'Gee, I apologized but Waldo won't accept it and he still won't forgive me. It looks like we are definitely going to have to counsel with Father Charlie.'

Suddenly, without comment, Waldo started walking away. Aroma panicked.

"Waldo, wait. We need to speak to Father Charlie. He can help us."

"I don't speak to humans. I don't trust them."

"Well, in that case I will do the talking and you can give your comments to me, and I will pass them to him."

As Waldo continued walking away he turned and emphatically insisted "I don't need anything from humans. Speak to him yourself".

"Waldo, wait! I need you to help me get back home safely."

"You got here by yourself. You can get home by yourself."

"But I was almost killed by your friend. At least get me out of wild boar country."

Silence...................!!
"Please! Waldo!! I have a family!!

By now Waldo was almost out of hearing distance. He stopped and turned to look in Aroma's direction. Aroma wasn't sure what it meant but realized that Waldo wasn't going to be his travelling companion and the risk of being killed was real once again.

"Well, I better get moving if I'm going to get home by sundown. I thought I would be here for the night but as it turns out I'm not safe now that Waldo is not around to protect me."

Aroma searched the perimeter of the clearing from his vantage point in the tree. The thought of running for his life from a charging wild boar was beginning to stress him once again. Seeing nothing threatening he climbed down from the tree to begin the most dangerous part of the journey. If he could make it safely to the other side of the clearing his chances of getting home alive were pretty good. He looked back one last time to see if Waldo was still visible. Waldo was nowhere to be seen.

12

Suspicion

Father John was in a hurry. It was the first Friday of the month and thirty retreatants would be arriving at 4PM for the monthly retreat. He was the official greeter and was responsible for setting up the welcome table at the main entrance. He still had to make copies of the program for this month's retreat and it was already 12:30. After finishing lunch he left the dining room and headed for the office to begin making copies. As he passed the superior's office and continued down the hallway he heard a voice call out,

"Oh, Father John, would you step in for a moment please?" Recognizing Father Mark's voice he turned around and walked back to his office.

"Good afternoon Father Mark."

"Father John thanks for stopping. I just wanted to report to you that Father Charles is scheduled to be released Tuesday morning. Would you like to be the one to pick him up?"

"Oh, sure Father Mark. That would be fine. What time should I be there?"

"Any time after 10 AM according to the hospital"

"I'll be there about 9:30 just in case they release him early" John assured his superior as he walked out of the office.

"Wow, Charlie isn't being released until Tuesday. I thought he would be released today or tomorrow. That means Aroma might show up for his meeting with Charlie and not be able to contact him. He might think Charlie has changed his mind and then he'll become discouraged and head home. I better rush those programs and get down to the valley and try to contact Aroma."

John was very concerned about Aroma. He was an animal with human characteristics and had revealed that all animals can speak. And while John and Charlie were unable to share that information with their peers, lest they be considered insane, he nevertheless knew that it was vitally important that Charlie keep the lines of communication open. Unfortunately, Charlie won't be available until Tuesday and Aroma might return at any time. He may have even been looking for Charlie these past few days while he was hospitalized. As John entered the office he was surprised to see Father Michael using the copy machine.

"Hi Mike. How long do you think you'll be? I need to make about forty copies of the retreat program."

"Probably about an hour; John. If you have something else to do I could make the copies for you when I'm finished."

"Gee, that would be perfect if you would. I need to get down to the valley for about an hour."

Looking at his watch John realized that he needed to hurry so he could be back by 2 PM. As he ran down the hallway to the patio garden he passed Father Mark's office once again. Surprised to see John running Father Mark stepped into the hallway to see where he was going. At the far end of the hallway John made a right turn and headed toward the garden. Father Mark was curious as to why he was rushing to the garden and stepped out on the terrace which overlooked the countryside and the valley below. Moments later John appeared and ran down the pathway to the valley.

"Why would he be rushing to Father Charles's hide-a-way" Father Mark wondered? 'Father Charles is in the hospital and Father John needs to set up for the retreat. He was going to print programs.' As he returned to his office he heard the copy machine making copies and wondered if Father John had left the machine on to make copies while he was gone. Walking to the office he saw Father Michael using the copy machine.

"Father Michael, did Father John say where he was going?

"Yes Father Mark. He said he needed to get down to the valley for about an hour."

Walking back to his office Father Mark could not contain his curiosity and decided to follow John to the valley and see what the rush was all about.

John quietly made his way down the pathway in an effort to avoid scaring Aroma should he be nearby. His plan was to stand on top of the boulder by the shed and call his name, hoping that he would respond. Then he could explain the situation so Aroma wouldn't think he had been double crossed. As he reached the valley floor he noticed fresh animal tracks in the vicinity of the large boulder and shed and wondered if they were Aroma's paw prints'. As John climbed to the top of the boulder, Father Mark began his decent down the pathway in the hope of observing Father John's activities.

"Aroma! Aroma, I need to speak with you. Father Charlie is sick and cannot meet with you right now."

Waiting 10 seconds for a response, which didn't materialize, John decided to raise his voice and be more insistent.

"Aroma, I need to speak with you, I have very important information for you!"

No response... at least not from Aroma. Father Mark responded however in wide-eyed disbelief as he stared through the shrubbery at what appeared to be one of his priests losing his mind.

"Aroma, that's the name of the skunk Father Charles said he spoke with. And now, Father John is calling him by name to report that Father Charles is sick. I don't believe this."

"Aroma, Aroma, where are you," John bellowed into the surrounding countryside. "I need to speak with you"!

Silence... and more silence... was the only response John could elicit from the animal kingdom.

"Well, I guess I'll have to try again tomorrow; for now I need to get back up the hill. The retreat starts at 4PM and I have work to do."

Father Mark stepped further into the woods and hid behind thick vegetation as John made his way up the hill. Hoping he wouldn't be seen, his plan was to confront Father John after dinner and get to the bottom of this very strange behavior. As John approached very near to his superiors position Father Mark moved closer to the ground and unintentionally stepped on a fallen branch which snapped with a loud cracking noise. Instantly, several birds flew away and

John froze. Father Mark held his breath and didn't move as John searched in all directions for the source of the noise. Seeing nothing, and becoming fearful, he bolted up the hill to the monastery. Father Mark breathed again, this time with a sigh of relief. As he emerged from his hiding place he walked very slowly back up the hill. He decided to take his time and give Father John a good head start so he wouldn't be seen. With the retreat scheduled to begin shortly this was not the time for an interrogation. That would happen later; of that he was certain.

13

Compassion

Aroma emerged from the tall grass with a sigh of relief as he looked back at Wild Boar country. He had made it safely across the clearing and through the heavy tall grass but decided this would be the last time. It was just too dangerous. From now on Waldo would have to come and visit him; that is if he ever could bring himself to a point of forgiveness. Aroma sensed that he had done all he possibly could to repair their friendship and now the rest was up to Waldo.

"Two more hours and I should be home, just before sundown. I hope that eagle isn't around, I still hurt from this morning."

With the river still between Aroma and his family the danger of a hungry bear or eagle was still a significant risk. As he approached the tall trees he knew the terrain would begin to go downhill for about a half mile until it reached the river bed. That would help him conserve energy. And with the day drawing to a close he was tired and needed all the energy he could muster. He had been up since dawn and still had about four miles to walk, or run, as the case may be. With the river bed in sight his enthusiasm propelled him faster down the hill as he broke into a run in the hope of shaving a few minutes off the journey. Suddenly he stopped dead in his tracks as he spotted a bobcat drinking at the river's edge.

"I don't believe this. I'm almost out of the dangerous territory and now I have to contend with a bobcat. Maybe if I go upstream a few hundred feet I'll be able to cross the river before he notices me. Once I'm on the other side, even if he sees me, he probably won't chase me; there is so much vegetation I could easily hide, and he knows it."

Quickly, Aroma raced through the tall trees moving two hundred feet up stream in the hope of safely crossing the river. Finding himself in an unfamiliar area he began to survey the river bed and the large and small rocks that he would have to negotiate.

"Wow! This doesn't look like a good place to cross; too many small rocks just below the surface. I need more large ones to stand on so I can jump from one to the other."

Looking further upstream Aroma could see an area of very large rocks interspersed with smaller ones. He could probably jump from large to small and make it to the other side without going in the water. Looking back at the bobcat he noticed he was just sitting on the riverbank looking toward the other side.

"Perfect. If he stays put I can run along the bank another hundred feet and start crossing."

Running at top speed Aroma turned to keep an eye on the bobcat and was shocked to see he was looking directly at him while still sitting.
Terrified he continued running toward his planned location for crossing without looking back. As soon as he reached his jump off point he turned to see the bobcat in a full gallop racing toward him.

"No! Please No! I'm almost home!"

Leaping from rock to rock Aroma knew full well

that bobcats will chase their prey into the water. Most cats avoid the water but bobcats are an exception. And being the size a large dog, with razor sharp teeth and claws, Aroma would be no match for this hungry predator. Half way across he turned to see the bobcat already in the water and running along the rocky bottom. Because he was much taller than Aroma he didn't need to jump from rock to rock and was seconds away from catching and killing him.

"No!! I don't want to die here. Please... Please God. If you exist... help me!"

Making one last effort to save his life Aroma jumped into the water and let the current pull him downstream. The big cat gave chase and was just about to dig its claws into Aroma when it suddenly stopped and put its front paws on top of a large rock. Aroma continued downstream a short distance and pulled himself up on top of a small rock and began running from rock to rock until he reached the other side of the river. Running toward the safety of the dense vegetation he turned to see where the bobcat was. Out of breath and exhausted he was amazed to see the bobcat still holding onto the big rock with its two front paws. Half its body was above water and the other half was under the water.

"Maybe its paws are caught between rocks on the bottom of the river. I hope so. That will give me time to get safely out of here"

Seizing the opportunity to escape Aroma began running towards home. Ten minutes later he paused to rest and collect himself from his latest brush with death. 'I wonder what will happen to that bobcat if it can't free its paws? It will either drown when it loses strength from holding onto the rocks, or a bear will see it and certainly kill it. Well…I can't help. If I try, once it is free it will surely kill me."

Perplexed, and somewhat undecided, Aroma continued towards home at a moderate walking pace. He tried to keep his mind on the landscape so he would travel in the right direction, but the thought of the bobcat's desperate situation wouldn't leave him. He remembered, in vivid detail, his own terrifying experience when the wild boar was chasing and trying to kill him, and how he was rescued by Waldo.

"I can't do this. I can't just continue toward home knowing the bobcat is facing certain death. He must be terrified. He's holding on to a rock and will soon lose his strength and drown. I have to help him."

Aroma spun around and began running back toward the river. Convinced that no one else would be attempting to rescue the trapped animal he knew that he was its only hope. But, would the dangerous cat, once freed, turn and kill him? That was the question that frightened him as he raced through the heavy vegetation which separated him from the river. Less than 10 minutes later, and out of breath, Aroma peered through the cover of the thick vegetation and was shocked to see Waldo standing on the opposite bank of the river directly across from the bobcat. Keeping behind the safety of the vegetation Aroma noticed that the bobcat was obviously weakening as the strong river current steadily pushed against him. Suddenly the bobcat spoke.

"Can't you at least give it a try?"

THE MONK & THE SKUNK 61

"No." Waldo responded. My hooves are very narrow and will easily get caught in the same rocks that are trapping you. I always go down stream where the river bottom is very sandy."

"But I'll drown if you don't help me. Besides, we just had three kittens and they will starve if I don't bring them some food. My wife died last week while protecting them from wolves that attacked when I wasn't home. She fought them off but then bled to death. Please... help me."

Waldo was silent. Aroma became agitated and from the safety of his hiding place yelled...

"Waldo... you let me cross the dangerous clearing by myself and now you won't help save this bobcat from certain death. What has happened to you? "

"I didn't let you cross the clearing by yourself... wherever you are. I was watching you the entire time."

"If that's the case then why didn't you help when the bobcat was chasing me?"

"Because you ran down the river bank and into the water so quickly I couldn't warn you. That is not a safe place to cross."

Seeing that the bobcat was losing strength rapidly Aroma bolted out from behind the vegetation and ran down the river bank. Positioning himself as close as possible to the trapped animal he offered conditional help.

"Look... you are going to die if I don't help you. And if I help you, you can then turn on me and kill me."

"No! I will not turn on you. I will not kill you."

"How do I know I can trust you? You're desperate and will promise anything. And once you are free, you can change your mind."

"NO! I will not change my mind. Please save me. I am sorry I tried to kill you. I just needed food for my babies. Please help me!"

"Waldo, I need you to protect me from this bobcat. Just walk slowly and carefully to the rock he is holding on to. I'll go under the water and try to free his paws. If I am successful and he attacks me, you can protect me."

Waldo was silent.

"Waldo… get over it. I already apologized to you. This is important and we are losing precious time. We can talk about your anger later."

Slowly, and with obvious reluctance, Waldo waded into the 2 foot deep water. As he approached the bobcat he gave him an extremely threatening look.

"Let me warn you mister bobcat. If you make one move to harm Aroma I will bite your head off; in one bite. Is that clear?"

"Yes! Yes! It is very clear mister boar, very clear."

Aroma jumped from the river bank to the first rock above the water. "Ok… I'm going to get to those rocks just upstream from you and go under water to see what the situation is. Then I will surface and tell you what we need to do. I think it would be a good idea if you prayed to God. I did and he protected me from you."

THE MONK & THE SKUNK

Aroma jumped into the river and went under to see how the bobcat's paws were trapped. The bobcat looked at Waldo and said "What is this God stuff?"

"I have no idea. You're asking the wrong guy."

Aroma surfaced. "Your left paw is between a small rock and a big one. If I dig some of the sand away from the small rock I might be able to move it enough to free your paw. Your right paw is between two big rocks and if you twist your leg enough you can free it. But you can't twist it because that is the leg supporting you. Once we free your left paw you can then stand on that leg and then you can twist your right leg and you will be free. Waldo, it would help if you also prayed to God."

"Hey! I'm not even talking to you yet and you're asking me to believe in someone named God. I never heard of him. He's probably someone that monk you have been talking to believes in. And we all know that humans are dangerous."

"Excuse me!! Would you guys mind discussing this later? I can't hold on much longer".

"Okay! Are you ready? I'm going under again and will try to move the sand away from the small rock by your left paw. When I tap your left leg pull your paw free. Then stand on your left paw and twist your right leg until you are able to free your right paw."

Aroma dove under the water again, and working as fast as possible, cleared the sand away from the small rock, moved it slightly and tapped the bobcat's leg. Immediately the cat pulled his paw free and stood on it for support as he twisted and pulled his right leg free. As Aroma surfaced and caught his breath he watched the big cat leap over the rock he had been holding on to and race towards shore. Holding onto the rock himself Aroma waited to see what the cat would now do. He was standing right where Aroma needed to go in order to get home.

"Thank you Aroma, I didn't think you would be able to save me but you did. I won't forget you for this. I will never chase you again"

"How about never chasing and killing any animals again? You can eat plants and fruits and vegetables. Waldo and I are both vegetarians and we are healthy and strong."

"I'll try."

Aroma and Waldo watched as the bobcat ran down stream to the sandy area and began crossing back to the other side. He had to continuously jump into the air because of the depth of the water. When he reached the other side Waldo yelled "What's your name"?

"Lightning"

"Why is your name lightning?"

"My dad told me it's because I am sort of yellow and very fast."

Taking one last look in Aroma's direction, Lightning bolted into the woods. He had been gone too long and was concerned for the safety of his kittens.

"Thank you for helping me Waldo. If you hadn't been here he might have attacked me. By the way, would you really have bitten his head off in one bite?"

"That was just a threat to protect you. I would never do something like that. But if he did attack you I would bite him just to scare him off."

"I appreciate your being here for me Waldo. But now I need to get to the other side and begin my journey toward home. It's getting late and I don't want to travel at night. Do you need me to help you backtrack out of here to the other side? I can see where the rocks are while you walk backwards." Waldo nodded a reluctant yes, choosing not to speak to Aroma. He still hadn't forgotten the hurtful experience heaped on him by his best friend. Carefully guiding Waldo's feet as he walked backwards Aroma was able to bring him safely to shore. Where Waldo would choose to go from there was unknown, but if he chose to follow Aroma he would have to go down stream to the sandy area where he had safely crossed many times before.

"Ok Waldo. I'm going to cross here where I have rocks to jump on. If I don't see you again I hope you at least remember that I'm still your friend."

Waldo didn't respond but started walking toward the sandy area. Aroma deliberately didn't watch. He knew how sensitive Waldo was and didn't want to discourage him from following him home. Quickly jumping from one rock to another he reached the other side and dashed into the underbrush. He still could make it home before sundown if he hurried and didn't have any more incidents to deal with.

14

Turmoil

Father Mark nervously tapped his fingers on his desk. In five minutes Father John would walk into his office and be compelled to explain his strange behavior in the Valley. He had been notified by Father Michael that he was to report to the superior's office immediately after the last retreatants where checked in for the retreat. And that would be just about 5 PM which would leave an hour of time for this critical meeting. At 6 PM Father Mark would need to leave in order to be in the main dining room to address the retreatants prior to dinner. At four minutes to five Father Mark could not quiet his racing mind as he struggled to decide on the wording for his first and most important question. 'What was Father John doing standing on a big rock in the valley, calling into the woods to inform a skunk that Father Charles was sick and couldn't meet with him as promised?' That question, by itself, was not the issue making him nervous. Following Father John into the valley seemed like an unjustified invasion of privacy. And if Father John was offended, it could lead to an uncomfortable discussion and a lack of trust in the future. Besides, Father Mark is the interrogator and the tables could turn if he doesn't phrase the question properly. As he continued his frantic search for the critical words he heard footsteps coming down the hall. 'Oh great, here he comes. I'll just have to go with whatever comes into my head.'

"Good evening Father Mark. Father Michael

THE MONK & THE SKUNK 67

indicated you wished to speak with me."

"Yes Father John, yes I do. I certainly do wish to speak with you. Yes I do. I uh…"

Father Mark was beginning to unravel. He couldn't think of anything to say that wouldn't reveal that he had followed John into the valley.

"Uh, please have a seat Father John. Make yourself comfortable. I asked you here so we could talk, as it were, and uh…"

John sensed the great discomfort that Father Mark was experiencing and shifted positions in his chair to distract from the awkward moment.

"Father John, how was your day? I noticed you were heading to the valley as I was walking on the terrace."

"Oh my day was hectic Father Mark. First I checked on things in the valley for Father Charles. Then, as you know, I had to man the welcome table for the arrival of the thirty retreatants."

"Checked on things in the Valley"?

"Well, yes. Father Charles will be returning on Tuesday and the valley is his special retreat."

"Yes, I am aware that the valley is his special retreat. But I didn't know that there was anything to check on, as you put it."

As Father Mark continued to avoid asking the incriminating questions, so did John avoid offering any more information than necessary.

"Uh… Father John, do you remember Father Charles telling all of us at lunch one afternoon that he had been talking to a skunk in the Valley?"

John sat straight up in his chair, suspicious that

the conversation was about to become very challenging.

"Yes I do, Father Mark."

"Well, then you probably remember that there was quite a bit of laughter after he said that."

"Yes, I do remember."

"Did you laugh?"

"No."

"Why not?"

"Because Father Charlie is my friend and I felt sorry for him. The entire community was laughing at him."

Father Mark was hoping their conversation would lead to an opportunity for him to reveal his presence in the valley. So far, John's cautious answers were preventing that from happening.

"Did Father Charles discuss his imagined conversations with you after the laughter subsided?"

"Yes, he did."

"What did he say?"

John was becoming anxious. If he answered every question Father Mark was likely to ask, he would, at some point, reveal everything Father Charlie was trying to keep secret.

"Father Mark, do you think it would be more appropriate to ask these question of Father Charles when he returns on Tuesday?"

"I will discuss it with him Father John. But I sense a need to discuss this situation with you also. I am concerned about Father Charles mental health. When someone tells you they have been speaking with a skunk named Aroma it deserves further

THE MONK & THE SKUNK

investigation."

John panicked. How could Father Mark know that the skunk's name was Aroma? Neither he nor Charlie had mentioned it to anyone.

"So after the laughter subsided, Father John, what did Father Charles have to say?"

"He was upset that the community had laughed at him. He wanted the opportunity to explain his experience, but, they laughed all the more."

"Did he relate his experience to you?"

"Yes."

Father Mark was becoming impatient. John was giving short answers and offering no information.

"Father John, why do I have to pull every bit of information out of you? You obviously know much more than you are revealing. You are forcing me, as your superior, to demand that you to tell me all about Aroma."

John was shocked. He looked directly at Father Mark and asked, 'How did you know the skunk's name is Aroma?

Father Mark was speechless. The question took his breath away as his face turned bright red. There was an embarrassing silence as the two priests stared at each other. While the uncomfortable silence continued John finally leaned forward toward Father Mark's desk and repeated the question.

"How did you know his name is Aroma?"

15

Abandoned

Waldo was growing impatient. He and Aroma had traveled to Father Charlie's hide-a-way on two separate occasions but Charlie could not be found.

"Look Aroma, I agreed to begin speaking with you just for the duration of this supposed counseling. But for two days your Father Charlie hasn't shown up and I say we either go and find him or I'm heading back to the high plains. I followed you all the way home just to make sure you made it safely. And we're not even friends anymore."

Aroma was in great distress. To convince a wild boar to do anything was an immense task. They are notoriously stubborn. But when you personally insult one it becomes almost impossible to communicate.

"Waldo, I'm really sorry about this. I guess we'll just have to head up the hill to the monastery and look for Father Charlie. I've only been up there once before and it was just to look through the window when they were attending Church."

"How close can we get to the buildings without being seen?"

"The path goes right to the outside garden and there are plenty of trees and bushes between us and the rest of the buildings in case we need to hide. Actually it's almost lunch time so if we just wait for the bell to ring we can look through the dining room windows and I can point out Father Charlie."

The unusual duo made their way up the dirt path to the outside Garden Gate. Waiting behind thick vegetation for the lunch bell to ring Aroma turned to Waldo and assured him that their meeting with Father Charlie would definitely take place.

"I know you're skeptical that our meeting will happen Waldo, but please, just trust me for a little while longer."

Bong… Bong… Bong, the lunch bell rang and echoed across the country side. Immediately Aroma began moving around the main building to the other side where the dining room was located. Waldo cautiously followed while remaining behind the tall and thick shrubbery. His frame was much larger than Aroma's and could easily be seen by the monks. Aroma whispered "Stay hidden until I call you. I'm going to run up to the windows and try to spot Father Charlie." Waldo silently nodded.

As the priests filed into the main dining room Aroma positioned himself next to a small window in an effort to remain hidden while he watched for Father Charlie to emerge through the door. Ten monks had already taken seats at various tables but he could not see Father Charlie. Suddenly he spotted Father John as he passed through the door and took a seat right next to the exit sign. Patiently waiting for Father Charlie, Aroma counted 26 monks seated and still no Father Charlie. At the head table a tall priest stood up and began to pray aloud as the other monks stood and joined in. Aroma became anxious. What if Father Charlie didn't show up? How would he explain that to Waldo who was running out of patience? The priest finished the prayer and everyone sat down and began eating. Aroma panicked as desperate thoughts raced through his mind.

"Should I try to get Father John's attention and signal him to come outside. If I don't do something fast Waldo will head back home and I may never see him again. I can't make that dangerous journey to wild boar country anymore. Fragrance and the kids were worried sick last time."

Without any signal to Waldo, Aroma ran to the end of the dining room windows so he could be as close to John as possible. Hoping to gain his attention without alerting any of the other monks, he stood directly in front of a clear window and began banging on the glass with his paw. The sound was barely audible. Running back to the shrubbery he frantically searched for a stick or small stone hoping to make enough noise to cause John to look in his direction. Finding a flat stone he bolted back to the window. 'I hope this works. But if the other monks see me I don't know what I'll do next.' Aroma began rapping on the window hoping to make enough noise without breaking the glass. Tap-Tap-Tap, but, still no results as the monks continued eating their lunch and conversing with one another. Suddenly Aroma started waving at John, followed by jumping in the air, but he was so small nobody noticed. As the sun streamed through the window the monks were oblivious to his presence until, without warning, Waldo appeared next to Aroma and completely blocked the sun's rays which had been shining in John's direction. Curious, John looked up and spotted Aroma standing next to Waldo. Stunned, he stopped eating and quickly looked to see if anyone else was aware of the animals' presence. So far he was the only one looking at the window. Without comment he left the dining room and ran to the outside garden. Noticing that Father John left before the thanksgiving grace that was prayed at the end of every meal, Father Mark stood to follow him. As he reached the door he saw John running at the end of the very long hallway and watched as he made the turn to the outside garden. Pushing the door closed he too raced down the hallway and made the turn for the outside garden. As he hurried to catch Father John he recalled their last conversation and how it had abruptly ended when he told him that he could not answer his question. John did not ask for an explanation as to why Father Mark could not answer the question 'How did you know his name is Aroma?' John had just accepted the fact that his superior was refusing to answer his question and there was nothing he could do about it. Now, Father Mark was racing to catch him in the hope of witnessing him calling for Aroma. He was quite sure that Father John would be so shocked that he would not question him further. He would just accept the reality that he was discovered and the cat was out of the bag, so to speak. Reaching the garden he caught a fleeting glimpse of John as he raced down the dirt path to the Valley. Waiting 60 seconds to give him a head start, Father Mark then charged down the path hoping to discover what the mystery in the valley was all about.

16

Surprise

John looked at his watch as he patiently waited in the main lobby of the hospital for Father Charlie to be discharged. "Five more minutes and Charlie will be a free man. I hope they're on schedule. They promised 11:00 AM and this hospital has a reputation for being punctual."

Suddenly the elevator bell rang and the door opened.

"Wow Charlie, the moment is here. How do you feel?"

"I'm very anxious to get home John. I miss the community and I miss the valley."

Minutes later as John turned the car out of the parking lot and onto the main highway Charlie asked him if he had been able to go to the valley as promised.

"I did Charlie, and I believe I was the only one to go down there. I tried to find Aroma to tell him you were in the hospital but he didn't answer me when I called into the woods. I just wanted to let him know that you weren't avoiding him. I was afraid that if he didn't have communication from either you or me he might get discouraged and never return."

"Good thinking John. He is a somewhat sensitive individual."

"When I returned to the monastery I had to man the welcome table for the retreat. And before I was finished at 5 PM Father Michael instructed me to report to Father Mark's office after the last retreatent

THE MONK & THE SKUNK

was signed in. When I walked into his office he was very nervous and had difficulty asking me questions about you and the valley. At one point he became annoyed that I was offering very limited information and demanded that I tell him all about Aroma. I can't imagine how he would know Aroma's name, but at the same time I saw it as an opportunity to turn the tables and I asked him how he knew his name was Aroma. He became embarrassed and refused to answer the question. He then dismissed me. That was Friday and now it is Tuesday and we haven't spoken a word to each other since."

"Doesn't sound good John; I'd better get down to the valley as soon as we get home."

"Its 11:55 Charlie, don't you want to wait till after lunch?"

"No. I really need to find Aroma. He probably thinks I've abandoned him."

As John pulled into the parking lot he dropped Charlie by the main entrance so he could take his belongings to his room.

"In case you change your mind Charlie, I'll be sitting by the exit sign in the dining room right next to the door."

"Thanks John" Charlie called out as he hurried into the Monastery. Twenty minutes later as the monks were eating lunch Charlie walked out of the monastery's main entrance and circled the building to the path which led to the valley.

"Gee, I don't have the strength for my usual entrance. Two weeks in the hospital has really weakened me. I'll just walk down the path and sit on the boulder playing my guitar and hope that Aroma will hear my singing."

Charlie had no idea that Aroma and Waldo were just ahead of him, anxiously waiting by the shed. They were expecting Father John to come charging down the path at any moment after having seen them through the dining room window. As Father Charlie approached the valley floor he began to sing Amazing Grace which immediately alerted Aroma. Running to the center of the clearing Aroma waited for him to emerge from the bushes while Waldo hid behind the shed. Suddenly Charlie reached the end of the path and stepped in to view.

"Charlie" Aroma shouted with great excitement. "I've been looking for you for three days."

"Aroma, what a pleasant surprise, I was worried that I would have to search for you."

"Where have you been Charlie? I really needed to speak with you?"

"I've been in the hospital for two weeks. I was just released this morning. I had a very serious case of pneumonia but I'm okay now, although very weak."

"I went to wild boar country and found Waldo. He's here with me now but is hiding until I tell him there is no danger. We came to counsel with you as you suggested."

"There is no danger Aroma. But I must ask you - am I safe to be around Waldo?"

"You are safe as long as you don't try to hurt me" a booming voice warned from behind the shed."

Aroma ran to Charlie's side. "Don't worry, that's

Waldo, he won't hurt you. He just wants to be sure you're not going to try and kill him. That's what humans have done to us for as long as we can remember."

"I will not harm him Aroma."

"Waldo, Charlie will not harm you. It's okay for you to join us now."

Slowly and very cautiously Waldo emerged from behind the shed. His immense size caused Charlie to panic as he backed up towards the path.

"It's okay Charlie", Aroma shouted. "It's okay; he won't hurt you... right Waldo?"

"I won't hurt you Charlie" Waldo responded with great assurance in his voice, as he walked closer and closer to Charlie.

Aroma noticed that Charlie was starting to tremble. "He's safe Charlie...really. Watch this."
Aroma ran to Waldo who was now only ten feet away.

"Watch this Charlie... shake Waldo". Waldo held up his hoof and Aroma extended his paw and the two shook hands. "See, we're friends"

"No we're not Charlie" Waldo insisted. "That was just to make the point that I'm not aggressive. We are not friends. That is a thing of the past. I'm here because Aroma wants to be friends again and he said you can help us. So I agreed to this meeting because he pleaded with me. And considering that we used to be good friends I've decided to do one last favor for him."

"Uh... okay. I understand. You used to be very good friends and now you are not. And we have planned on counseling, so now that you are here we can begin. Do I have that right Aroma?

"Yes Charlie. You are correct."

"Okay, I will go to the boulder and sit down and the two of you can place yourselves where ever you are most comfortable."

As Charlie and Aroma walked toward the boulder Waldo objected. "Excuse me! Father Charlie and I have not been introduced to one another."

"Oh Waldo, I'm sorry. Yes, we need to have introductions. Father Charlie this is Waldo and Waldo this is Father Charlie."

"I'm pleased to meet you Father Charlie" Waldo offered as he stepped closer to the trembling monk.

"Thank you Waldo. I am happy to meet you also."

"Relax Charlie. It's safe. Trust me. Right Waldo, everyone is safe, right?"

"Right Aroma, everyone is safe."

As Aroma and Charlie climbed on top of the boulder, Waldo stood beneath the large tree directly next to them.

"Well gentlemen I believe it would be appropriate if I prayed before our counseling begins. And I always begin prayer with the sign of the cross. So when I raise my hand to my forehead I say 'In the name of the Father' – then I move my hand to my chest and say – 'and of the Son' – then I move my hand to my left shoulder and say – 'and of the Holy' – then I move my hand to my right shoulder and say – 'Spirit' – then I move my hands together and say - 'Amen'. If you noticed that is actually making a cross as I make the moves with my hand."

"Why do you make the sign of the cross? Waldo

and I are unfamiliar with that".

"Well, we can get into that at a future meeting, but for now I will just say a prayer and then we can listen to what you and Waldo would like to discuss?"

"Uh, sure, we can do that... right Waldo"?

Waldo nodded.

"Now I will pray. Our Father, who art in Heaven, hallowed be Thy name. Thy kingdom come, Thy will be done, on earth as it is in Heaven. Give us this day our daily bread and forgive us our trespasses as we forgive those who trespass against us. And lead us not into temptation but deliver us from evil, Amen.
I'm finished with the prayer. Now we can begin our discussion."

"Charlie, as I mentioned to you two weeks ago, Waldo and I had a falling out. And I want to be as reasonable about this as possible, so... because I have already told you my side of the situation I think it would be only fair to let Waldo go first."

"Waldo, I am happy to listen to anything you have to say and I won't interrupt you. You may speak as long as you like. And Aroma I ask that you do not speak until Waldo has finished."

"I won't speak. I promise".

Waldo was encouraged by the opportunity offered to him to speak his mind. He walked to the center of the clearing, turned and faced Charlie and Aroma. Just as he was about to speak there was a sudden pounding of feet and rustling of bushes as someone was racing down the path to the valley. Waldo spun around as Aroma yelled, "Don't worry Waldo it will be Father John". Instantly John burst into the valley and came to a screeching halt just 20 feet from Waldo.

"John" Charlie called, "it's okay. This is Waldo, he's a friend"

Waldo slowly backed up, unsure of what to expect from Father John who stood frozen in position. Suddenly there was a new sound coming from the top of the path. More pounding feet as someone else was rushing to the valley.

"Who's that?" Aroma yelled as he jumped off the boulder and stood next to Waldo.

"I don't know" Charlie shot back, causing Waldo and Aroma to charge into the woods as Father Mark burst through the bushes and landed right next to John. Charlie stared in silent disbelief as his confreres stared back ... equally speechless.

17

Pleading

Waldo had just finished a friendly dinner with Aroma, Fragrance, and their little ones, under the big tree which they call home. Much of the conversation had been about Aroma's trip to wild boar country. But now, as the sun was beginning to set, Waldo unexpectedly announced that he would be leaving at sunrise and heading home.

"Waldo, wait! You have to give me a chance to arrange a private meeting with just Charlie, you, and me. I have no idea who that other person was who was rushing to the valley, and we didn't stick around long enough to find out. I'll try to get Charlie to come here, to my home, but you need to give me at least a few days."

"I've already been here three days Aroma. I have a family too and I need to get home. I'm sure they are beginning to worry about me."

"Well, I'm sure they don't have to worry as much as my family needs to worry about me. I'm very small, but you are huge. There are practically no predators that would dare attack you."

"My greatest concern is humans. The hunting season starts next week and we boars are a prime target. Every year they invade our territory and kill some of us."

"Well, then you are safer here Waldo. This isn't boar country."

"I have a family to protect. When the hunters

get close to us I attract their attention by running through the woods and drawing them away from my family. Those of us who are killed are usually the fathers."

"Today is Tuesday Waldo. If the hunting season doesn't start until next Monday you could stay at least until Thursday and leave Friday morning. It takes less than a day to get home, which means you will spend Friday night with your family. That will give you plenty of time to prepare for the hunters."

"I've already been here longer than expected, I'm going to leave in the morning."

"But, Waldo! This is very important."

Waldo was silent and walked away from the large tree in order to watch the sunset. Aroma began to panic and immediately consulted with Fragrance hoping to discover a way in which to convince Waldo to change his mind.

"Let me talk to him" she suggested. "He's mad at you for spraying and insulting him, but he has nothing against me."

"Sure honey. Give it a try."

Fragrance approached Waldo as he was silently catching a last glimpse of the setting sun.

"Hi Fragrance; I was just marveling at how the sun always sets in the west and always rises in the east. I don't know why it doesn't set in the South or the North but I'm sure there must be a reason. Humans with all their books probably know the answer."

"Waldo, I wanted to speak with you about Aroma. He's been very upset for months about the situation between the two of you. He knows he offended you and he has made an honest effort to apologize. He doesn't understand why you won't forgive him. And that is what he was hoping could be resolved by counseling with Father Charlie. If you just give him two more days I'm sure he will be able to arrange a meeting with Father Charlie. If you leave now he fears that you will never come back. And returning to boar country, for him, is just too dangerous. Would you consider staying until Thursday?

Waldo looked respectfully at Fragrance, then at Aroma and the youngsters, and responded barley above a whisper; "I'll sleep on it… and let you know in the morning."

18

Interrogation

Anxiety filled the air as the priests silently filed into the conference room. Those to be interrogated sat on one side of the very large table, while those who would conduct the investigation sat facing them on the other side. The profound silence greatly intensified the apprehension as two very nervous priests and three administrative priests took their seats. The meeting was scheduled three days earlier, the first of its kind in the history of the monastery. The suspense and gossip for the past three days was enough to cause Father Charles and Father John to become sleepless. They were the unfortunate priests who were about to be interrogated by the administrators. Father Mark, the Superior, greeted the two defendants and extended the same greeting to his fellow interrogators, Father Michael the Vicar and Father Andrew the director of ministry.

"Good morning my brother priests, Father John, Father Charles, Father Michael, Father Andrew, let us begin with prayer. 'Dear God our Father, by the power of your Holy Spirit, and the saving grace of your Divine Son, Jesus, we ask for your guidance as we proceed with this investigation. We seek the truth and ask for your blessing upon us so that the truth will be made know and accepted by all. We pray in the name of your son, Jesus, Amen'. Father Mark then looked directly at Father Charles and Father John, remembering clearly their encounter 3 days earlier in

THE MONK & THE SKUNK 85

the valley. He had rushed down the dirt path and as soon as he emerged from the bushes he noticed a large and a small animal running into the woods. Demanding an answer as to why they were in the valley, and why the animals ran away, he was shocked to hear their explanation and their obvious belief in the insanity of their answers.

"Father Charles, I will begin with you and ask that you repeat for the benefit of Father Michael and Father Andrew exactly what you presented to me as an explanation for your presence in the valley this past Tuesday.'

Charlie sat straight in his chair and took a deep breath to gain his composure and diminish his anxiety.

"Father Michael, Father Andrew, for you to have a better understanding of why I was in the valley I will need to give you a little history of this situation. Several months ago I was in the valley, playing my guitar, when a skunk started speaking from behind the bushes. I ran back up the hill, somewhat afraid and somewhat disbelieving. The next day I returned and the same thing happened, only this time I saw the skunk and began speaking with him. He can actually speak like a human. He told me his name was Aroma.' Father Michael and Father Andrew began to shift in their chairs and break eye contact with Charlie. He immediately sensed their disbelief and tried to reassure them that he was telling the truth. 'Father Michael and Father Andrew, please let me finish before you reach any conclusions. That same day I embarrassed Aroma and he ran back into the woods. He actually exhibited human behavior. I shared this with Father John, and although he was faithful as a friend he really didn't believe any of this. He thought I was having emotional problems. The next day we went to the valley and after a half hour of calling Aroma and then going through woods looking for him, it seemed we would not find him. At that point Father John decided to return to the Monastery. As he was beginning to leave Aroma suddenly appeared and spoke with us. He indicated he wanted to counsel with me and that he would return on another day when he was more prepared. He also insisted that Father John not be present and that our conversations be completely confidential. A few days later he appeared in the valley and we conversed for half an hour. I actually counseled with him and gave him my best advice. He has a problem which I am not at liberty to reveal because of my promise and commitment to keep it confidential. He indicated at the end of our counseling session that he would return and discuss the results of his implementing my advice. The next day I was taken to the hospital with pneumonia. Two weeks later upon returning from the hospital I went directly to the valley looking for Aroma. He was there waiting for Father John who he had alerted through the dining room window. He was surprised to see me and complained that he had been looking for me for three days. Just as we were beginning to speak with one another Father John came running down the path and appeared in the clearing right in front of us. Ten seconds later Father Mark arrived and the animals disappeared."

"What do you mean when you say 'animals'?

Father Andrew asked.

"Well Aroma had a friend their also, but I'm not permitted to reveal his name."

"Was he also a skunk?"

"I'm not permitted to reveal that either."

Father Michael looked at Father John.

"Father John, are you under any constraints of confidentiality with the skunk or skunks?"

"No"

"Who or what was the other animal?"

"His name is Waldo and he is a wild boar."

"Did you speak with him?"

"No. As soon as I arrived, Father Mark was right behind me and Waldo and Aroma ran into the woods."

"Father Charles, did Waldo speak with you?"

"I am not at liberty to say."

There was a moment of silence and Father Mark spoke. "Father John did you hear Aroma speak?"

"Yes, I did."

"Do you believe everything to be just as Father Charles has stated."

"Yes I do"

"Father Charles, Father John, I give you a direct order. You are prohibited from going to the valley until further notice. I will discuss this matter at length with Father Michael and Father Andrew. Depending on the outcome of our discussion I may order you both to undergo psychiatric evaluation."

Charlie and John appeared very somber as Father Mark led the priests in a closing prayer. As the two of them departed the meeting room the remaining administrators began their discussions.

"What do you think John? Did they believe any of my testimony? "

"I don't know Charlie. I don't see how they can completely discount it because I too attested to the facts as you stated them. If it was just you saying these things they might consider you to be mentally ill. But I agreed with everything you said and they have to deal with that. This will be very interesting to see what they decide. But in the mean time what are you going to do about Aroma and Waldo?

"I don't know John. The situation is serious. Aroma really needs my help. I can't abandon him like this but I'm prohibited from going to the valley. I'll just have to pray and hope that he finds me."

19

Indecision

"Father Michael, there must be something more to your answer than just uncertainty. I understand that you can't make up your mind as to whether they are telling the truth or whether they are mentally ill. But are you not leaning in one direction or the other?

"Father Mark, I don't think it is a simple case of mental illness. After all, Father John and Father Charlie are saying the same thing. They didn't both lose their minds at the same time. And the animals did run away when you arrived, but were remaining there with Father John and Father Charlie before you scared them away. That doesn't mean that I believe the animals can talk. They could just be friendly animals."

"If that is the case, then would you say that Father Charles and Father John are lying about the animals being able to speak?"

"That is a possibility but I can't imagine why they would tell such a lie. This just doesn't make sense, and that is why I can't make up my mind one way or the other."

"Father Andrew believes they are telling the truth, I think they are lying, and you can't make up your mind. I have prohibited them from returning to the valley and that should effectively bring this situation to a close. But we still won't know the truth. And that disturbs me. Father Michael, your office is near the path that leads to the valley. I want you to keep an eye on that path and the valley in general. If you see either, Father Charles or Father John venturing in that direction I want to know about it immediately. Is that understood?

"Yes Father Mark. I understand and will do as you have ordered."

20

Mysterious Help

Waldo quietly approached Aroma's home just before sunrise. He had struggled all night with indecision, waking up and falling asleep several times. But now, with the first light of dawn inching its way into the valley, he was eager to tell Aroma that he had decided to stay until Friday morning.

"Good morning everyone, it's me, Waldo."

Because life in the animal world is very dangerous, it is important to identify yourself. There are no police to call if an intruder is at your door. If you are small, you hide. If you are big you defend yourself.

"It's ok Aroma, it's me Waldo, come on out."

"Good morning Waldo. I was just about to go looking for you. Have you decided what you're going to do?"

"I have, and for you it's good news. I'm going to stay until Friday, if necessary. But I want to have an understanding with you. We will waste no time in finding Father Charlie, and when we find him we must insist on an immediate counseling session. In 48 hours I leave, no matter what."

"Wow! That's the best news yet. Thanks Waldo. And I agree with your deadline."

Aroma ran inside to say good bye to Fragrance and the kids and in seconds he emerged ready to go.

"Let's go Waldo. I'll lead the way."

Racing through the valley Aroma led Waldo down familiar paths hoping to find Charlie in his hide-a-way. But the fear of Charlie not being there became more pronounced the closer they got. Twenty minutes into the half hour journey Aroma stopped to catch his breath.

"Waldo, if Charlie is not at the hide-a-way we'll have to go up the hill to the monastery again. Right now the priests are probably arriving in the Chapel. We should be able to look through the windows and hopefully get his attention."

Waldo nodded agreement and Aroma continued toward the hide-a-way at a running pace. They had only two days to find Charlie and repair their friendship and Aroma didn't want to waste a minute. As they made the last turn on the path Aroma was able to see through the trees to the clearing and discovered that Charlie was not there. Racing through the clearing he charged up the hill to the monastery with Waldo right on his heels. As he reached the top of the hill Aroma was looking directly at the gate to the outside garden.

"Ok Waldo, here's the plan. You stay behind the bushes until I find out where they are. I'm going to check the chapel first and if I find them I'll run back here and get you. I'm too small for them to see but they can't miss you. When we get to the chapel we'll try and get Charlie's attention. If we're successful he'll come out to meet us in the valley. However, if the other monks see us they'll come with Charlie and we'll have to hide in the woods. When they leave I'm sure Charlie will stay and we can speak with him then."

"Sounds good, but hurry, we have very little time."

Aroma raced around the outside of the main

building until he came to the stained glass windows of the chapel. Jumping up onto a window ledge he looked through a small clear section hoping to see the monks filing into the chapel for morning Mass. Only one monk was in the chapel and he was sitting at the organ. Several minutes passed when suddenly the organist started playing the entrance hymn. As Aroma looked to the rear of the chapel he noticed several priests processing down the main aisle with the rest of the monks following behind. Searching through their ranks he spotted Father John followed by two other priests and then Father Charlie. He waited for them to take their seats so he would have a place to point to when Waldo arrived. As soon as they were in position he jumped from the ledge and raced around the monastery to the path where Waldo was waiting.

"Let's go Waldo, the coast is clear."

Waldo stepped from behind the bushes and followed Aroma to the Chapel. At 400 pounds he was an imposing sight, guaranteed to scare away any human and most animals. When they reached the chapel Aroma jumped on to the window ledge and pointed out Charlie to Waldo.

"I see him Aroma, but he's looking to the front of the church and won't notice me at this window. I need to move to a different window, closer to the front, and then he might see me."

Waldo moved to a window opposite the altar and looked back at Charlie who was in the middle of the chapel. Hoping to gain his attention, without alerting the other monks, he stood in front of the window and blocked the sunlight with his immense size. Aroma began waving at Charlie from his vantage point but Charlie was absorbed with the message being delivered by the priest who was speaking from the pulpit.

"We read again and again in sacred scripture of the great mercy of Jesus. Surely one of the most profound moments in Our Lord's life was when he asked His Father to forgive those who were crucifying him. As they were driving the nails into his hands and feet he said 'Father, forgive them, for they know not what they do.' If Jesus could forgive those who were killing him, should we not also forgive those who persecute us?"

Waldo looked in Aroma's direction, ready to ask who Jesus is, when he found Aroma already looking towards him.

"Who is Jesus?"

"I'm not sure but I think he's God."

"Well, if he is God why did the priest call him Jesus?"

"I don't know."

The priest continued speaking.

"In the Sermon on the Mount we read of Jesus saying 'blessed are the merciful, mercy shall be theirs.' If we look to God for mercy, than surely we must be merciful to others. Just as he forgives us we must forgive others."

Waldo stared at the priest and then at Aroma. Quietly, without comment, he moved away from the window and began walking towards the path to the valley.

"Waldo, what's up? Where are you going?"

THE MONK & THE SKUNK

Without responding, Waldo continued to distance himself from Aroma.

"Hey, what's going on? Waldo, wait."

Aroma jumped off the window ledge and chased Waldo.

"Waldo, you said you would stay until Friday. Why are you leaving? We still have two days."

Waldo was unresponsive as he approached the top of the path to the valley.

"Waldo... you can't leave now; we need to counsel with Father Charlie. Please, keep your promise. You said you would stay until..."

Waldo spun around and looked directly at Aroma.

"I hear you Aroma, I hear you. You don't have to keep repeating yourself."

"Ok, ok... but why don't you answer me?"

"I don't know. Something is happening, but I'm not sure what."

"Do you mean the priest?"

"No. I mean me. Something is happening with me."

"Are you getting sick?"

"No, I'm confused. I was anxious about our counseling and I was anxious about my need to get back home and protect my family. But now I'm confused. I don't know what to do next."

"Well don't leave before we talk with Father Charlie. This is too important. I think we better change our approach and be more aggressive in our efforts to contact him. I'm going to go inside the monastery and hide in the hallway and wait for Father Charlie to pass by. I'll try to get his attention without the other priests noticing me."

Aroma ran to the outside garden gate which he had noticed in the past was never completely closed. Worried that Waldo would head back to the high country he realized that he needed to find Charlie and find him fast. Reaching the gate he rejoiced to find it open. He quickly bolted into the outside garden to begin his frantic search for an open window or any other place in which to gain access to the inside of the monastery. Finding the door to the monastery closed he searched the many windows and found the top of one small window above the grape trellis open. Wasting no time he began climbing the trellis causing many of the vines to break under his weight and scatter grapes on the ground. Undeterred he continued upward until he reached the window and jumped to the ledge. Looking inside he realized there was nothing to step on to, which left him only one option; drop to the floor eight feet below. Risking a broken leg, Aroma let go of the window top and landed on his feet inside the monastery. Pain shot through his very sensitive paws which were accustomed to the soft earth and not suited for tiled floors. Instantly he began running down a long hallway hoping to find the way to the dining room. Once there he planned on hiding behind anything big enough to conceal him and wait for the priests to pass by on their way to breakfast. How he would alert Father Charlie without the other monks hearing him was still a mystery. But with time running out he needed to try anything.

21

Paralyzed

"John, did you see Waldo at the window?"

"I did, and I also noticed Aroma at another window. I wanted to rush out and speak with them but Mass was more important."

"True... plus we didn't want to alert the others and answer endless questions. We need to figure out a way to contact Aroma without going to the valley. Father Mark didn't prohibit us from communicating with him or Waldo."

"We might not have to Charlie; it looks as though they're trying to contact us."

As Charlie and John continued walking from the chapel to the dining room they were preceded by most of the other monks. Two however had remained behind in the chapel when they departed; the organist, Father Phillip, and the Superior, Father Mark. As they made the last turn they entered the main hallway of the monastery. At one end was the entrance to the lobby and offices, and at the other end was the dining room. Adorning both sides of the 100 foot passageway was an impressive collection of sculptures of the saints in Heaven. Midway to the right was the corridor that led to the outside garden; to the left was the hallway to the monks' individual rooms. Just as they were about to pass the intersection a voice yelled, "Charlie wait!" Stopping instantly they looked around to see who was calling them, and discovered no one.

"John, did you hear that?"

"I did, but I don't see anyone".

By this time all of the other monks had entered the dining room.

"Charlie, it's me Aroma"

"Aroma, where are you."

"I'm behind the statue; the one with the bird on its shoulder. I'll come out if the coast is clear."

"The coast is clear…"

"Hold it Aroma", John whispered! Don't come out… here comes Father Mark."

Father Mark and Father Phillip reached the main hallway and headed towards the dining room.

"Not having breakfast today my brother priests?"

"Oh, good morning Father Mark; yes we are having breakfast. Father John and I just stopped for a little discussion."

"Better come along now gentlemen or you'll be late for Grace."

John and Charlie obediently followed Father Mark to the dining room as Aroma watched from the safety of his hiding place. As soon as they entered the dining room, and the door closed, Aroma dashed across the hallway and ran down the corridor to the outside garden.

"I don't believe this. I finally made contact and that other priest showed up again. I have to find a way out of here and tell Waldo to be patient. I know he promised to stay until Friday but he has been acting a little strange."

Reaching the door to the outside garden, Aroma found it closed. Rushing around the corner to the room with the open window he frantically looked for

THE MONK & THE SKUNK

anything to climb on.

"Nothing! Not one thing in this entire room that I can use to climb on. I better yell for Waldo and hope no one else hears me. **Waldo**...can you hear me? Hey...Waldo! Waldo I'm in the monastery and can't find a way out. Go to the dining room windows and try to get Charlie's attention. Waldo, did you hear me?"

Aroma quietly waited for the much needed response but heard nothing. Trying one final time and still experiencing the same silence he realized he needed to get back to the statue and wait for Charlie to pass by as he returned from breakfast. Fortunately, Waldo had heard Aroma but didn't answer for fear of the Monks. Getting home to protect his family was paramount and anything that would prevent him from getting there was to be avoided.

"I hear you Aroma but I can't answer. Humans kill animals. I'll try to get Charlie's attention but if they all come running out of the monastery, I'll run to the valley and hide."

As Waldo approached the dining room he noticed a large clear window near the far end of the building. Peering through the glass he realized that he was adjacent to the table where Father Mark sat. Recognizing him as the priest that charged into the valley and scared him and Aroma away, he made every effort not to gain his attention. Looking elsewhere, and hoping to see Charlie, he scanned the entire room. Suddenly a priest stood up and pointed directly toward Waldo and started yelling. Abruptly the other priests all turned and looked in amazement causing Waldo to panic and run from the window. Immediately, Father Mark bolted from his table and charged to the door, followed by 24 curious priests. As they raced down the hallway towards the outside garden Aroma positioned himself as far as possible into the niche behind the statue. As the stampede passed his hiding place and the priests entered the outside garden on their way to the valley, the door to the dining room quietly opened.

"John we need to find Aroma fast. I hope he's still behind that statue of Saint Francis. Some of the priests might not go down to the valley and they'll return here any minute."

Aroma's keen ears heard the conversation fifty feet away and he jumped from behind the statue landing in the middle of the hallway.

"Charlie, you have to counsel with me and Waldo today. He's going back to the high country to protect his family during the hunting season. He leaves Friday morning and that gives us only two days to save our friendship."

"Aroma, the other monks might be back any minute. You have to get out of here. We need to figure out a meeting place. Fr. John and I have been prohibited from going to the Valley."

"Ok. Just tell me where."

"On the north end of the property, the opposite side from the Valley, there is a sitting area with benches next to a replica of the Pieta. That is a statue of Jesus and Mary. I can meet you there at night. In the daytime we will be seen. I'll be there after dinner tonight."

"Ok! I'll meet you there and so will Waldo if he hasn't been scared off by the priests. But you'll have to get me out of here. I can't open any of these doors."

"Follow me. We'll go out the side door of the chapel."

Aroma followed Charlie to the chapel as Fr. John headed back to the dining room. When they entered the chapel Aroma curiously studied everything he saw before they reached the side door.

"Aroma, you better go to the edge of the property and circle around to the valley through the woods or the other priests might see you as they return for breakfast."

Aroma dashed through the door and ran to the edge of the woods while yelling back to Charlie, "See you tonight."

22

Hope

Waldo charged down the path to the valley followed by 25 curious priests. Reaching the boulder he hid behind the vegetation hoping they wouldn't search further and cause him to run even deeper into the woods. In the last hour since leaving the window at the chapel his interest in counseling with Father Charlie and Aroma had increased. He and Aroma had been friends for many years, and while Aroma's offense was painful and unjustified, it didn't necessarily have to bring about the end of their friendship. Waldo was still mad, still hurt, and still not inclined to forgive. But for some reason, which he couldn't explain, he now wanted to try and save their friendship. As he pondered what he would say in counseling, he suddenly heard the voices of many priests approaching the valley. As they marched down the path he moved a little further into the woods and waited. The first to appear was Father Mark, followed by half a dozen monks. The remainder seemed to be staying at the top of the path.

"This is where I saw that wild boar running into the bushes with the skunk. He's probably gone further into the woods again, although this time I didn't see the skunk. Did you see the skunk at the window Father Michael?"

"No Father Mark, but like you I did see the boar, as did everyone else."

"I hesitate to chase after him. We don't know if he's dangerous, and I'm unfamiliar with the woods.

I don't understand why he was looking through the window."

"There is always the possibility that he was looking for Father Charlie."

"Father Michael - that would make sense if the boar was able to speak. But Father Charles has not indicated that the boar can speak. Even if he had I wouldn't believe it. And I certainly don't believe the skunk can speak as Father Charles has insisted."

As the priests were talking Aroma made his way through the vegetation and arrived at the side of the clearing just in time to hear Father Mark announce his disbelief in Aroma's ability to speak. Remaining silent and out of sight he waited to see what the priests would do next.

"Gentlemen, we need to get back to breakfast. Father Michael, continue in your observance of the outside garden and the pathway to the valley. If you see Father Charles or Father John venturing near the valley I want to be informed immediately."

"I understand Father Mark. I will do as you have requested."

As the monks made their way back up the pathway to the monastery, Aroma continued toward the clearing hoping to find Waldo. He needed to explain the plans for their meeting with Charlie. This was the moment he had been waiting for and finding Waldo was critical.

23

Encounter

The setting sun glistened through the dining room windows as Grace after dinner was prayed aloud by the monks. When completed they filed out, one by one, leaving only Charlie and John sitting at a table.

"As soon as it's dark I'll need to get out there and wait for them John. You need to keep watch and alert me if anyone is venturing outside. This is a very important meeting and I don't want Waldo and Aroma scared away."

"I will Charlie, but if anyone goes for a walk I have no idea in which direction they will go. They may walk down to the road or even to the Pieta. But I'll warn you if they are getting close. That's the best that I can do under the circumstances."

"Ok John, but whisper a warning as loud as you can without anyone else hearing you. I'm going to my room. As soon as it's dark I'll climb out of my window which is very near the Pieta. I'll wait for Aroma and Waldo as long as it takes."

Heading to his room Charlie passed Fr. Michael in the hallway. Nodding a friendly greeting, and receiving one in return, he continued toward his room wondering if Father Michael believed him. He hadn't indicated one way or the other.

"Ok, let's see, I'll need some bug spray and a small flashlight in case I have to signal Aroma that the coast is clear. I hope he understands and doesn't think

THE MONK & THE SKUNK

it's a warning. I'll only use it if he doesn't show up after an hour. He may be waiting for some sign indicating that it's safe to leave the woods."

Twenty five minutes later Charlie opened his window and climbed out onto the grass. Looking in both directions for any sign of the other monks he closed his window. Walking to the Pieta and the benches he looked back at the monastery 100 feet away and could see that most of the room lights were on. He had purposely tuned his off so he would not be visible climbing in and out of the window. As he sat down to wait he gazed at the beautiful replica of the Pieta. Given to the monastery by a benefactor it was the same size as Michael Angelo's Pieta and was also sculpted in white stone with great detail just like the original. As he looked at the face of Jesus he could sense the suffering he went through. Now dead, and lying on the lap of his mother, Jesus seemed to be calling Charlie to silent prayer.

"Lord, please help me to understand the meaning of your creation in the animal world. Aroma and Waldo can speak and they are hurting from a relationship problem. I have no idea how to help them other than to give them the same advice I would give to a fellow human. I don't know if they will live after this life, and I don't know how to explain that to them if they ask. Still, they seem to exhibit the same emotions that human's exhibit. In my heart I want to help them even though they are animals."

Suddenly there was a rustling in the shrubbery near the benches. Then a very quiet voice whispered

"Charlie is it safe. I'm in the bushes and Waldo

is still in the woods."

Charlie spun around, "Aroma, yes it's safe. Tell Waldo."

Aroma ran to the edge of the woods and seconds later Waldo emerged from the bushes and followed Aroma to Charlie.

"Welcome Waldo, Welcome Aroma. I'm very happy to see you both. Because we don't know how long it will be safe here we should begin counseling right away. Waldo you were about to tell your side of the story when we were interrupted in the valley. Would you like to begin with that now?"

Waldo stepped closer and was about to speak but hesitated. "Uh yes, I would like to discuss that; however, there has been a slight change in what I want to say. This all goes back to Aroma offending me, completely out of the blue, for no reason that makes sense, and then expecting me to just forget about it. But now, in light of an unexpected experience, I want to modify my position somewhat."

Charlie and Aroma listened with great interest but were completely in the dark as to what Waldo's unexpected experience was. Afraid to interrupt for fear he would be offended, they chose to remain silent.

"So Charlie, I need to ask you a few questions."

"Sure Waldo, go ahead."

"What did it mean when the priest said at Mass this morning that Jesus forgave those who were crucifying him?"

"Jesus was a human being and he was killed by crucifixion on a cross. They drove nails into his hands and feet and raised him up on a cross. But his love for them was greater than their offense and so he forgave them."

"Aroma said that he thinks Jesus is God"

"That is true. Jesus is God."

"Who is God?"

"God is our creator and the creator of all things. He loves us and wants us to be with him forever in Heaven, a place of light, happiness, and peace. But because we are sinners, and don't deserve to be in Heaven, He chose to pay the price for our sins by suffering on the cross. If we are sorry for our sins He forgives us and we can go to Heaven to be with him forever."

"Just you, or can animals go to Heaven also?"

Charlie was speechless. He didn't know the answer and didn't want to hurt Waldo or Aroma. Waldo didn't wait for the answer he sensed was not going to materialize.

"Humans kill animals. Does God forgive them?"

"God forgives sin"

"Is it a sin to kill an animal?"

"I don't think so, but I'm not sure. I think if it is for food that someone needs in order to live, then it would not be a sin. But if it is for sport, then I think that might be sinful."

"Aroma was very mean to me and I have been having a difficult time forgiving him. One day, for no reason at all, he sprayed me with that foul smelling stuff that he sprays other animals with when they attack him. I have never insulted him or offended him in anyway. I was hurt by his sudden attack and sensed that our friendship was not what I thought it to be. He said it was just a joke and that he was only kidding. When I got home my poor family had to suffer from that horrible smell for several weeks. And now, because he apologized, he expects me to just forgive him like it was no big deal. Well, it is a big deal and I am still very much offended.

"Well thank you for sharing that with me Waldo. Aroma would you like to speak now?"

"Uh, no thank you Charlie. Waldo pretty much presented everything as it was. But I do want to emphasize that I have apologized many times to Waldo and he still won't forgive me."

"Waldo, do you feel comfortable sharing with us the unexpected experience you mentioned earlier?"

"Yes, I do Charlie. I will share that with you.
Aroma, forgiving you was not something I had considered. Your offense, whether a joke or whatever; was a complete surprise and uncalled for. You had no right to treat me that way. But, in hearing Charlie's explanation a few minutes ago, I now understand that Jesus forgiveness came from his love for those who were killing him. His forgiveness wasn't based on their deserving it. So I realized that your apology couldn't be the basis for my forgiving you because it wouldn't wipe away the offense. The offense is still there. So my forgiveness must come from my love for you, but, I'm not sure that I still love you. Unfortunately, the longer I don't forgive you the more painful it becomes to live with this situation. I have the desire to forgive; however, I'm still hurt, I'm still offended, and I want some time to think about all

of this. But, for now, I have to get home. My family is in danger. Father Charlie I want to come back and talk some more in the future. Thank you for listening to me."

"You're welcome Waldo. Thank you for being here. I look forward to seeing you again. Before you leave I want to clarify one thing. God is perfect and when he forgives he wipes the offense away. It no longer exists. We, his creatures, have memories and it is difficult to wipe things out of our memory. But our love for one another can overpower the effects of our memory and bring peace to us when we forgive."

Waldo turned and began walking toward the woods.

"Thank you for counseling Waldo. Please come back my friend."

Waldo didn't answer Aroma as he silently disappeared into the dark woods. Aroma looked at Charlie; "I hope he comes back. He still hasn't forgiven me."

"Aroma, look at this sculpture. It is called the Pieta. It is a depiction of Jesus lying dead on the lap of his mother Mary. He had just been taken down from the cross on which he died. His suffering, which he willingly accepted in order to save us from our sins, is proof of his love for us."

"If Waldo ever forgives me will that mean that he loves me again?"

"Probably...but you'll have to ask him to be sure."

24

The Price of Love

Aroma paced back and forth inside his tree home as he related his counseling session to Fragrance. This was the second time she had heard the entire details but she didn't complain. She could see that Aroma was extremely concerned about Waldo's safety and if he would ever return. Although he had indicated to Father Charlie that he wished to return and counsel again, nothing guaranteed he wouldn't change his mind. Then of course this was the hunting season, and there was always the remote chance that Waldo would be killed as were two of his friends in recent years. But Waldo was extremely fast and experienced so Aroma discounted that as a possibility. Guessing where Waldo would be at this very moment Aroma reasoned that he would be close to home.

"I'm sure he would have spent the night in the woods and left for home the first thing this morning. It's almost noon and he should be crossing the river right about now.

What Aroma didn't know was that Waldo decided to take the highway instead of traveling through the woods. This would cut his journey time in half and get him home before dawn. Waldo knew it was dangerous because of the traffic but the shoulder was wide with soft grass to walk on and he could always run into the woods whenever he saw automobile headlights approaching. Having safely reached home before dawn he was now preparing his family for their annual struggle to stay alive. With less than four days before the start of the hunting season they rehearsed over and over again their plan for survival. Monday morning, at dawn, they would walk a half mile from their home and separate in the woods, making sure to keep each other in view about 100 feet apart. If the hunters spotted any family member, that member would warn the rest and Waldo would then charge toward the hunters scaring them into a defensive retreat. He would then turn and run in the opposite direction causing the hunters to give chase. In the mean time the family would run home and remain safe. This had worked well in previous years. Only one time did a hunter actually chase Waldo and shoot at him. The bullet hit a tree directly next to Waldo but he kept running and the hunter eventually gave up the chase.

For the next three days they practiced their survival strategy, and now as Sunday evening drew to a close the family prepared for a good night's sleep. Waldo struggled with the idea of praying to God but was unsure of the words and still unsure if he believed in a God he could not see. Instead of prayer he decided to speak from the heart as his family quietly listened.

"I don't know what the morning will bring. We know that humans have guns and that they kill animals. And they may kill some of us. If that should happen I want you to know how much I love you. If I am shot I won't be able to speak with you again. So I thought I better say it to you now."

Waldo's wife silently wept as she hugged her two little ones. Waldo walked closer and hugged them all. He was tired of this yearly threat to their existence, and was determined to find out from Father Charlie why God lets this happen. After all, if God is love, then he should protect Waldo and his family. Hours later, as the family slept, Waldo struggled to close his eyes. He knew the danger and he knew the risks. Running from one group of hunters could cause him to run right into another group who might kill him. As the night passed he was able to close his eyes for only two hours before the first light of dawn crept into the woods. Slowly he climbed out of their burrow and looked into the still darkened woods. Looking back at his sleeping family he quietly thought, 'God if you are real please protect us.' Minutes later everyone began to awaken and one by one joined him in a hurried breakfast of healthy green leaves from various plants. Minutes later, as they finished what could be their last meal together, Waldo announced... "Ok family; let's begin to move in the direction of the highway. That is where the hunters will be coming from. This will keep them away from our home so they won't know where to find us next year."

As Waldo and his family fanned out they kept at least a 100 foot distance between one another. Slowly they moved in an easterly direction with Waldo to the north and his wife to the south. With about two miles between them and the highway they would walk for about a half hour and stop. That would keep them a safe distance of 1 mile from the highway and there they would wait until sundown. Twenty minutes into their steady walking Waldo suddenly heard voices in

the distance. Looking in the direction of his family he signaled for them to be silent. That meant that no one would move or communicate. Suddenly the voices went silent and then…BANG!! … A loud shot rang out in the distance echoing throughout the woods. A boar was heard squealing followed by two more shots.
Then silence. "No", Waldo silently thought. "That's my Brother Bob's territory. I hope it's not him or his son Randy. They are the only males in the family who would run near the hunters."

Waldo continued walking toward the highway. They needed another ten minutes to safely distance themselves from their home. As he quietly moved further east he became extremely anxious for the safety of his family. Minutes passed and they were about to stop when he heard hunters approaching. Searching the heavily wooded area he spotted two hunters walking toward his wife. She was 100 feet from him and the hunters were another 100 feet from her towards the east. They were moving west at a good pace.

"I have to move fast. I'll head south east and then charge. This will keep them occupied so they won't see anyone else. Then I'll run towards the highway and hope they'll chase me."

Waldo began to run through the woods, dodging one tree after another. Not yet at a charging speed he still made good headway as his hoofs snapped the many fallen branches from the trees alerting the hunters. Then as he closed in on the men with the guns he began to charge, making loud snorting sounds as his speed increased. Completely surprised to see a mammoth boar in a full charge coming directly at them, the hunters ran in separate directions as Waldo approached. Suddenly, as they had their backs to him, he turned and ran in the opposite direction. Frantically trying to save his life he zigzagged through the trees making him a difficult target to hit. BANG! BANG! Two shots chased him through the woods, one hitting a tree next to him and the other screeching past his head at the speed of sound. Galloping at full speed he knew that soon he would be out of sight. BANG! ...A burning bullet ripped through the back of his right shoulder and exited out the front hitting the tree he was approaching. Blood splattered in his right eye blinding it. His heart pounded as he fought to keep up his running pace and gain enough distance between himself and his killers so he could rest and survey the damage. He had run so fast he was almost upon the highway and had to turn and head north as if he was going back to the monastery. Out of breath he stopped to determine if he was going to die or if he was only slightly wounded. With limited vision he discovered that the blood was running down his right leg but slowly enough that he thought if he rested it would stop and then he could continue. But he was still too close to the hunters so he continued running for another five minutes before stopping. Exhausted, he lay on his left side and tried to clear his right eye of the dried blood. Without paws he had to use his knee which was also covered with blood and proved to be ineffective. Continually blinking he was able to clear his eye enough to see that the wound was still oozing blood but at a reduced rate. His mind raced back to his encounter with Lightning and his description of his wife bleeding to death after an attack by wolves.

"God, if you exist please help me survive. I need to protect my family... I don't want to die. I know I will someday, but please, not now."

The traffic on the highway increased as the sun inched its way into the clear blue sky. One after another cars and trucks roared by, making it impossible for him to hear any approaching hunters. Trying to rest and regain his strength, Waldo searched for possible solutions to his dilemma. If he remained where he was there was a good chance the hunters would find him. If he started walking again the movement of his shoulder, with every step, could cause him to hemorrhage, and then he would surely die. Determined to do everything possible to survive, he struggled to stand but the pain in his shoulder made it almost impossible. Finally on his feet he searched the woods for his killers. Fifty feet of dense vegetation between him and the highway reassured him that passing motorists and hunters would never spot him. Looking south and west the woods seemed clear. North, was the direction back to the monastery and possible help? If he could get a message to Aroma there was a chance that Aroma would tell Father Charlie and maybe the priest would come to his rescue and stop the bleeding. But how much damage was done to arteries and veins was unknown. Waldo needed help, and fast.

"God, if you can hear me, if you are really there, I need help. I can't move or I'll bleed to death. If I don't move the hunters will probably find and kill me. I tried to protect my family and they shot me. I need to get a message to Aroma."

Waldo continued standing, silently staring into the woods. His mind played over and over again his joyful memories of life with his family.

"I don't want to die here. Please help me someone!!"

Looking to the sky, he desperately shouted in a loud voice… "Aroma"! Then, regretting the outburst for fear of alerting the hunters, he settled back down on his left side and waited. In moments his loss of blood, and weakness, put him to sleep as the sun advanced in the sky.

25

Questions

John and Charlie watched the last priest leave the dining room. With a half hour remaining before they would begin their daily routine, this was a needed opportunity to discuss Charlie's secret meeting.

"John, as you know, I am not at liberty to discuss any particulars. That was my agreement with Aroma. But the fact that I was meeting with them was no secret to you. They both showed up as scheduled and we had a serious discussion which, I believe, was productive. What the outcome will be I don't know. We'll just have to give it some time. But while their current situation is important, I believe there is a much larger question here. And it doesn't involve just them. It involves all of the animals in God's creation. Because of my experience with Aroma, and now Waldo, I have been struggling to understand the animals' position in God's plan."

"What do you mean?"

"I mean God's plan for the animals eternally. Do they have souls? Do they go to Heaven? Some people say the animals behave instinctively and some people say the animals act out of love. If they act from a position of love, and I don't know that they do, but if they do, then that means, I would assume, that they have souls."

"Why"?

"Because the love that we receive, and the love that we give is kept in our souls. All love comes from God. And God, as we know, is love itself. He gave us our souls when he created us. When we are receptive to His love we now have love to share. It is His love that we keep in our souls and share with others. Without a soul I don't understand where an animal could store God's love which he or she would share."

"Do you mean like when our dogs love us?"

"Exactly!"

"Do you really think that is love, or just instinct?"

"Giving love is a choice. Instinct is a reaction. A mother dog will protect her young instinctively. But it is love when she snuggles up next to them. Gorillas pick parasites off the fur of their mates. That is love."

"Are you sure about all of this?"

"No John. I'm not sure. To prove God's existence to someone is difficult. But to believe in God as an act of Faith is easy. In Faith, I believe that animals express love. But I can't prove it. Some people we meet in our lives don't express much love. Even members of our own community right here at the monastery. They have personalities that are different from mine or yours. But that doesn't mean they don't have love and at times give that love to others. And if we question them I'm sure they will tell us that they do in fact love. But the animals don't talk to us like our friends do so we assume they don't love. Now, with this revelation from Aroma and Waldo that all animals can talk, it offers us a tremendous opportunity to ask them if they love."

"And if they do, you say they have souls?"

"I do".

"The same kind of soul we have?"

"I don't know".

"We need to research this further Charlie".
"How about you do that John? Maybe one of your Theologian friends can enlighten us."

26

Unexpected Visitor

Waldo was laying motionless, sound asleep, fifty feet from a busy highway. The bleeding had almost completely stopped but the excessive amount of loss had left him exhausted. As the wind drifted through the tops of the tall trees it caused a slight rustling of leaves, a sound which was very familiar to Waldo. But an especially loud rustling awoke him and caused a sense of panic. Could it be the hunters and the moment of his death? Painfully raising his head, he looked in all directions. Seeing nothing, he lowered his head to the ground hoping to ease the pain in his wounded shoulder. Reflecting on his last meeting with Aroma and Father Charlie, he remembered the Pieta and Father Charlie saying it was Jesus and that Jesus was God.

"Jesus God, if you can hear me, I don't know what to do. I need help. If the hunters don't find and kill me I'll probably die here anyway. The dream I had while I was sleeping was really disturbing. I imagined Aroma and his reaction after learning that I had died, and how upset he would be because I had never forgiven him. I do forgive him but I've been reluctant to tell him for fear he might think his offense wasn't that bad and then he'll do it again. But, now it's too late to tell him anyway. I'll probably be dead soon."

High above in the tall oak trees, Waldo heard a loud commotion as two birds seemed to be fighting. Struggling to look up without moving his head he noticed a mother bird pushing an egg toward the edge of the nest. Another bird, almost identical in appearance to the mother bird, was objecting and pushing the egg back toward the center of the nest. Waldo assumed the other bird must be the male because of its slightly larger size. Suddenly the mother bird began to frantically flap her wings as if to attack the male. As he turned to move away she forcefully pushed the egg out of the nest. Waldo watched as the egg plummeted to the ground, crashing on top of a large rock and splitting in two. Instantly the male bird flew to the rock and pulled the egg pieces apart as he inspected the tiny bird that had been inside. Seeing that it was dead, killed from the crash, he began to weep and sing a strange bird song that was sad for Waldo to hear.

"Why did you do it, why did you do it", he repeated over and over. Standing close to the tiny dead bird he hung his head in silence and remained motionless for several minutes. Quietly the mother bird flew down landing next to the male.

"I told you, we already have two eggs ready to hatch in a few days. We can't take care of three."

"Yes we can. I could have built a bigger nest, but now it's too late; our baby is dead. I wanted to teach it how to fly, and now I can't. I'll never forgive you."

Instantly the mother bird flew away and returned to her nest. Waldo was disturbed and wanted to comfort the father bird who was still mourning the dead baby, but he didn't have the strength. Beginning to stress about his own situation he worried... "I can't stay here, but I'm too weak to leave. Maybe the father bird would be willing to help. He can't see me behind these bushes but he can fly higher and see that I'm not a threat." Struggling to raise himself up from behind the bush, he called to the bird. "Hello… hello I need help. Will you help me?"

Abruptly the bird flew to a high branch and looked down on Waldo. "What happened to you, you're covered with blood?"

"I was shot by hunters, and now I'm too weak to walk because I have lost so much blood.
I need to get help from humans at the monastery."

"Where is the monastery?"

"It's on the other side of the river, at the north end of the valley."

"I don't talk to humans, they will shoot me."

"You can go to my friend Aroma and ask him to speak to them. He lives in a tree house about two miles west of the river."

"What does Aroma look like?"

"He's a skunk".

"I need to bury my baby first. It won't take long."

Suddenly, there was another load rustling of leaves followed by the snap of a branch. Waldo panicked, thinking the hunters had found him and in moments they would mercilessly kill him. Laying down and closing his eyes he hoped they would pass without noticing his large grey body. Anxious minutes ticked by and still nothing. Opening his eyes again he watched the father bird dig a shallow grave with his feet, and then drag his tiny baby with his beak, gently pushing it into the grave. Curious about the rustling of

THE MONK & THE SKUNK

leaves and now a snapped branch Waldo picked up his head and looked in all directions. Shocked, he spotted a bobcat staring directly at him just twenty feet away. Although partially hidden by a thin bush Waldo sensed he had seen the animal before.

"Who are you? I see you looking at me."

Silence…!

"You can come out from behind that bush. I can't hurt you, I have been shot. Who are you?"

"I am Lightning mister boar."

"Lightning?"

"Yes, my name is Lightning. And I can't come out from behind this bush because you threatened to bite my head off in one bite. Remember?"

"I was just trying to scare you so you wouldn't harm Aroma. I would not bite your head off. But if you had harmed Aroma I would have bitten you just to frighten you away. But you have nothing to fear from me now. And please, feel free to call me Waldo"

"Who shot you?"

"Hunters; this is the beginning of Wild Boar hunting season. I was trying to protect my family and they chased me. I think they also might have shot my brother or his son Randy. Now I'm worried that they will find me and finally kill me. If I can get help from humans I might live. I've lost a lot of blood but if I walk to the monastery for help I will start bleeding again. So if help doesn't come to me I'll probably die right here."

"Maybe I can help. Where is the Monastery and where is your friend Aroma. I heard you calling him?"

"Aroma lives two miles west of the river and the

Monastery is another mile from Aroma's home at the north end of the valley."

"I know where the river is and I'm willing to try to find Aroma's home but I can't guarantee I'll be successful. Plus, I have to cross wild boar country and I just came from there. It's a risky journey, especially crossing the clearing. If a boar catches and kills me my little ones will starve."

Just as Waldo was about to answer, the father bird flew to a limb just above Waldo's head.

"Suppose I go with you Lightning and check the clearing before you cross it? The boars can't catch me."

"Well, yeah. That would be great. In fact if you make the complete journey there would be other times you could warn me of danger ahead."

"Ok, I'll do it. When do we leave?"

Before Lightning could answer Waldo painfully raised his head, "You better leave soon or I'm going to die. I need water to replace the loss of blood but I can't go get any."

Lightning agreed and looked at the bird… "If we are going to travel together I need your name."

"My name is Target."

"Target… why is your name Target?"

"My mom said I take too many chances around humans and therefore I'm an easy target."

"Ok Target. Lead the way. Keep me a safe distance from the hunters."

As Lightning and Target started to leave, Waldo pleaded… "Wait!! I might be dead by the time you return. Lightning, please tell Aroma I forgive him. If I

THE MONK & THE SKUNK

die before I see him I don't want him to suffer never knowing if I forgave him."

"Sure Waldo, I'll tell him".

As Lightning and Target disappeared into the woods Waldo anxiously looked toward the sky and pleaded… "Jesus God, please help me."

27

Dominion ?

John and Charlie had spent the last two days discussing creation and God's plan for the animals and mankind. Without reaching any absolute conclusions they nevertheless agreed on one important point. Humans have been given dominion over the animals, the birds, and the fish of the sea. But just exactly what God meant when he said "dominion" was not completely clear to them. John had contacted his friend Father Damian, who was a professor of theology at a university in Rome, in the hope of getting a more precise understanding of man's relationship with the animals.

"He just drove in the driveway John."

"Great, let's greet him at the door and walk him to the conference room."

Father Damian was considerably older than John and Charlie, both of whom were in their thirties. Occasionally he would be a guest homilist at the retreats held at the monastery. Today, however, he would hopefully be an advisor to John and Charlie who were uncertain as to how to proceed in the future should Waldo and Aroma return seeking advice.

"Good morning Father Damian, welcome once again to the monastery."

"Good morning Father John and Father Charlie. I always enjoy driving to the country and getting out of the busy city for a change."

As the priests walked down the hallway to the

conference room the discussion began to touch on the topic at hand. Finally seated at the table Father Damian asked, "I understand that you are uncertain about the meaning of the word "dominion" Father John, but you haven't told me why this has become so important to you."

John looked at Charlie hoping he would answer, sparing him the embarrassment of informing his long time friend that the two of them have been talking to animals who talk back. Charlie instantly picked up on John's anxiety and replied, "We've been talking to a skunk and a wild boar and they both have complained of humans killing animals. Therefore we need to know what God meant when he said "Be fertile and multiply; fill the earth and subdue it. Have dominion over the fish of the sea, the birds of the air, and all the living things that move on the earth."

Father Damian seemed shocked at Charlie's blunt statement, and for a very long five seconds silently stared at him. Charlie shifted in his seat, anxiously waiting for a response.

"Father Charlie...would you repeat that please. I'm not sure I heard you correctly."

John took a deep breath and moved to the edge of his seat.

"Uh, Father Damian, Charlie said we have been having conversations with the animals."

Father Damian gradually sat back in his chair, speechless, with a look of confusion settling into his face. John felt faint and cast a desperate look in Charlie's direction.

"That is what I said Father Damian. I was the first

to speak with the skunk. And now I am also speaking with a wild boar who is a friend of the skunk. Father John has spoken with the skunk but not the boar."

"I see. Uh...ok, you have been talking to animals and you want to know what God meant when he said have dominion over the birds and the fish and the animals. Is that correct?

John smiled, "Yes Father Damian that is our most important question although we have others."

"Others, what other questions do you have?"

"I can answer that John. Father Damian, do the animals go to Heaven? I was talking to Aroma and Waldo two days ago and they both were interested in knowing if animals go to Heaven."

"Are they members of the community here?"

"Oh, sorry; no they are not priests, they are the two animals I have been speaking with. Aroma is the skunk and Waldo is the Wild Boar."

Father Damian started to smile. "Forgive me gentlemen; I'm having difficulty keeping a straight face. This is not a joke I trust?"

"No Father Damian, Charlie is telling you the truth. I understand your doubting, but please trust us. Everything we are telling you is the truth.

"Ok Father John, I will give you the benefit of the doubt for the time being. But I will reserve final judgment until the end of our conversation. Now, will you please explain to me how and when all of this began? And what do you mean when you say you are speaking with the animals? Do they actually talk like humans?"

"John, I think it would better if I answered that.

I want to make sure that everything that is supposed to be held in confidence does in fact remain confidential."

"Sure Charlie, go ahead."

For the next hour Charlie gave a compete history of his and John's experiences with Aroma and Waldo. Father Damian seemed surprisingly interested and kept notes as Charlie covered every detail that he felt he was free to reveal.

"And so, Father Damian, that is where we stand at this moment. Waldo has returned to the high country and Aroma is praying that he will return in the near future so they can continue counseling."

Father Damian pushed himself away from the table and sat back in his chair. Gazing at his extensive notes, he looked curiously at the two younger priests.

"Am I to understand that the two of you are completely serious and that you absolutely believe everything to be as you have described it?"

John and Charlie spontaneously nodded in the affirmative.

"In that case I have no choice but to believe you. I'm not really comfortable saying that, but neither one of you appears to be insane, and I don't sense that you are lying. Therefore I'm compelled to take the next logical step and ask you to prove to me that the animals can talk. I realize that Waldo is out of town, so to speak, but what about Aroma?

"Aroma lives locally Father Damian. At the other end of the valley to be specific. But it isn't necessary for us to go to his home; he visits the hide-a-way on a regular basis. At the moment, however,

John and I are prohibited from going to the Valley, so we have been relying on Aroma to come to the Monastery. For the past few nights he has met me at the Pieta and we have briefly talked about Waldo. He also discusses, at length, the animals' relationship with God. Unfortunately, I have very little information to share with him. And that is why I asked Father John to contact you in the hope that you could enlighten us about God's plan for the animals in creation. We don't know if they have souls, or if they ultimately go to Heaven, or if they can actually love. Aroma is very intelligent and his questions are good questions. I just don't know how to answer him."

"I'm not certain how much help I'm going to be Father Charles; however, I do have some initial thoughts which I will present to you now. And when I return home I will spend some time researching these significant questions. If, and when, I discover something of substance, rest assured I will share it with you as soon as possible. My first impression is that God loves all of His creation. As you both know, God is Love. And from our experiences with God's love we know that He does not choose to love one minute and not the next. Humans do that, but God does not. When he loves us, or his animals, or the trees, or the stars, His love is consistent. He loves the animals far more than we do or ever could. He created them, so of course he loves them and wants what is best for them. His plans for us, eternally, include bringing us to Himself at the end of our earthly life. Does he have the same plans for the animals? I don't know. The most curious question of all is... 'Do the animals love'? Do they express love? If they do then I don't see why they would not have souls. The soul is that special place where love resides. And if they have souls, does that mean that they will go to Heaven? Those are very interesting questions for which I have absolutely no answers. But, as I mentioned, I will be researching this during the next few days and then I'll get back to you. For now those are my initial thoughts. As for meeting Aroma and experiencing his ability to talk like a human, I will need Father Mark's permission to be here in the evening. Should we speak with him now or do you want to discuss it with him privately?"

"Charlie and I will have to discuss it with him at his convenience Father Damian. He really wants us to forget this situation altogether. He doesn't know of Charlie's meeting Aroma in the evenings and this could present a problem. We will pray and discuss it and call you when we have permission for you to meet with us and Aroma."

"I will be praying for you my brother priests. If, in the mean time, the situation changes in any significant way, please keep me posted."

John and Charlie walked Father Damian to the entrance and waved goodbye.

"I don't know about you Charlie but I'm not looking forwarded to going to Father Mark about this."

"Don't worry about that John. I'm the one who has been meeting Aroma. I will assume that responsibility."

"Good. The sooner the better, I really want to get

this out in the open. Did you notice how Father Damian's conclusions about the animals and their relationship with God were similar to our conclusions?

"I did John. And that is encouraging. I hope his research agrees with us. Aroma really needs some answers."

28

Racing Against Time

Target searched the clearing from one end to the other. At three hundred feet above the ground he could clearly see the mile long and quarter mile wide danger zone. Lightning waited patiently in the safety of the tall grass, afraid to move without a sign from Target. Gliding to a low tree branch just above Lightning, Target whispered, "its ok. I don't see any boars in the clearing or the nearby grass. You should be safe to cross. I'll fly above and just ahead of you. If you see me suddenly fly in a particular direction it will mean that I see something I need to investigate. At that point you should stop moving and stay close to the ground."

Afraid to speak, for fear of the boars, Lightning nodded to Target and stepped into the clearing. Looking carefully in both directions he bolted across the danger zone and raced toward the safety of the tall grass on the other side. Half way across Target was still directly ahead of him and continuing to fly in a straight line. Confident he was safe, Lightning continued running at top speed and charged into the protection of the tall grass. Looking up for Target he spotted him standing on a high branch and waving him on. Eager to make it to Aroma's home in record time Lightning raced through the tall grass until he reached the flat ridge which separated the high country from the Valley. Moments later he began the descent to the river below. Target flew into the clear sky above the river, searched for danger, and flew back into the woods adjacent to the shore and waited for Lightning. Several minutes later, and needing a rest, lightning galloped down the hill to the river's edge. Trying to speak and catch his breath at the same time, he looked up toward Target and asked if the coast was clear.

"So far, but as you know this is eagle country. They can catch and kill both of us. That's why I remained in the woods. When you are ready to cross I'll fly to the other side searching in all directions. The eagles can be in any of the trees and are very difficult to spot."

"I need a rest but Waldo is bleeding to death so I'll just have to keep moving. I'm going down stream a little bit to the sandy area. It is the safest place to cross."

As Lightning ran down the river bank Target flew to the other side of the river and began flying up and down the tree lined shore searching for any eagles waiting in the cover of the woods. Seeing nothing suspicious and confident that Lightning would be safe he waved him on to the other side. As lightning ran and jumped through the water, Target flew to a low branch to discuss their next move.

"Wow, the current is strong today, but I made it without any problems. I need to rest a moment Target."

"While you're resting we can discuss where we go from here. This is the edge of the valley and Aroma lives one mile south of the monastery. The monastery is at the very northern end of the valley. So I'm going to have to fly into the center of the valley and then

THE MONK & THE SKUNK

South while keeping track of any land marks so I can find my way back here and lead the way for you."

"Sounds good Target. I'll wait in the woods a little way in from the shore so I'm not seen by any of the eagles which regularly patrol the river. That way I can rest and regain my strength for the final run."

Target flew due west making sure to stay below the tree tops so as not to alert any hawks, especially the large eagles. This was strange country for him and birds usually fly in numbers when leaving their home territory. As he ventured further into the woods the density of the trees and foliage became lighter making it easier for him to see greater distances ahead. Making sure to remember landmarks as he proceeded, he suddenly spotted what seemed to be an animal trail which ran north and south. Assuming this might be a well travelled route, he flew north directly above the narrow dirt path hoping to find the monastery. Flying for what he assumed to be half to three quarters of a mile he spotted a clearing with a shed and large boulder on one end and a path leading to the top of a hill on the other. Suspecting this to be the end of the valley, he flew above the trees and instantly discovered the monastery sitting on top of the hill in the bright sunshine. Making a quick circle of the property he noticed a tent being erected next to a statue and workers putting out rows and rows of chairs.

"This must be the monastery. But I can't waste any time here, Waldo is dying. I'll fly south one mile and hopefully locate Aroma's home."

Following the path South, Target spotted the point where he had turned north.

"Another quarter of a mile or so and I should see a large tree with an entrance at the base."

Less than a minute later he noticed two small skunks playing in a clearing near a large tree. Assuming he had found Aroma's home he flew to a low branch above the skunks.

"Excuse me! Is this Aroma's home?"

Unafraid of a small bird, but obedient to their parents instructions, one of the skunks answered "we are not allowed to speak to strangers".

"You don't have to speak with me. Just go to your parents and tell them that Waldo has been shot and needs Aroma's help"

Immediately the young skunks ran into the tree house and told their parents the shocking news. Rushing out the door, Aroma looked up to the small bird.

"I'm Aroma. What's this about Waldo".

"He's been shot by hunters. He desperately needs water because he has lost so much blood. Only humans can help him. Waldo asked lightning to find you and tell you to speak with the priests at the monastery and ask them to save Waldo's life. "

"Lightning"?

"Yes, Lightning the bobcat. He said he knows you. He is down by the river waiting for me to return. He had to rest because he ran all the way from the highway to the river. I flew ahead to find you so I could show Lightning the way."

"I need to get to the monastery but the priest I

THE MONK & THE SKUNK 137

know is not allowed to meet me in the valley. I usually only see him at night on the Monastery property. Will you fly to the monastery and speak with him and tell him what has happened?"

"No! I don't trust humans. They'll try to kill me. But I'll fly back to the river and get Lightning. He can run almost as fast as I can fly. We'll be back in no time at all.

29

Thin Ice

Father Charlie took a deep breath as he nervously approached Father Mark's office door. This would be the moment of truth. Either Father Mark would believe him or he would be sent to a psychiatrist for evaluation. There didn't seem to be any other options.

"Good morning Father Mark. I wonder if you could spare a few minutes. I'd like to discuss something with you."

"Good morning Father Charles. Yes, please come in and make yourself comfortable. I always have time for my brother priests. What is on your mind today?"

"Father Mark, you have instructed me, and Father John, to no longer go to the valley. Your reason was to prevent us from meeting with the animals who, we claim, speak with us. Both Father John and I have been obedient to your instructions."

"Wonderful Father Charles, I knew I could rely on both of you to practice your vow of obedience. And I'm sure you have realized the benefit of your obedience. We all know that animals can't talk, and by breaking your habit of going to the valley I'm certain that, by now, you understand this was all in your imagination".

Charlie panicked. He knew that Father Mark was about to dismiss him with a pat on the back and send him on his way.

"Uh... Father Mark... You didn't prohibit us from talking to the animals, you only prohibited us from going to the valley. I have been talking to the animals at night, by the benches, next to the Pieta."

Father Mark was stunned. In silence he stared at Charlie. His face became pale as his eyes darted in all directions searching for a response he couldn't find.

"The animals want to know if they can go to Heaven. They want to know why humans kill them for food when they themselves are vegetarians. I am currently counseling two of them and one has gone home to protect his family during hunting season. I have spoken with Father Damian who has offered to research information on animals and whether they have souls and…. "STOP!! That is enough Father Charles. You are in obvious need of psychiatric care. I order you to your room until further notice. You may emerge for meals and Mass and prayer but the rest of the time you are to remain in your room. I will make an appointment with the psychiatrist and inform you of the date and time. You are dismissed."

Shocked and dismayed, Charlie walked down the long hallway heading for his room. "Dear Lord I don't know what to do. Aroma needs help, Waldo needs help, and I need help".

As soon as Father Mark sensed that Charlie was a safe distance away he immediately dialed the university to speak with Father Damian. While he was waiting for the phone to be answered he wondered how much information Charlie had given him regarding the animals. If Father Damian was willing to research the possibility of animals having souls it must have been in response to a general question. Surely Charlie would not have shared his imagined experiences with Father Damian, for if he had Father Damian would certainly not have believed him. Nor would he have agreed to research anything and participate in this bizarre fantasy.

"Yes, hello, I'm calling for Father Damian in the theology department."

"One moment please"

As the phone rang Father Mark tried to decide on the proper approach in his questions to Father Damian. Should he ask what Father Charles had actually told him?. Should he ask how the research is going? Should he ...

"Hello, this is Father Damian".

"Good morning Father. This is Father Mark at the monastery."

"Oh, hello Father Mark. You beat me by about ten minutes. I was just getting ready to Call Father John to see if he had cleared my nighttime visiting with you."

"Nighttime visiting"?

"Well, uh yes. He has spoken with you I trust?"

"Actually no Father Damian, I have not been speaking with Father John."

"Oh, excuse me...I assumed that was the purpose of your call."

"No, however I will discuss that with you now if you wish."

"Well, I don't want to interfere with Father John's schedule, I'm sure he will be speaking with you shortly. May I ask the reason for your call?"

"Yes, certainly; Father Charles has indicated you are doing some research for him and I am curious as

THE MONK & THE SKUNK

to how it is proceeding."

"Oh, I see. Well it seems you are familiar then with our discussion. At the moment I have not uncovered any information about the status of animals in the divine plan other then what has already been revealed. The central questions I have posed in my research are; do animals have souls, do they enjoy Heaven with us, and do they have the capacity to love. While doing my research, several additional and somewhat interesting questions emerged. Are there good animals? Are there bad animals? Do animals forgive? Hopefully, if and when I actually witness the animals speaking with Father Charles, I will be able to ask them significant questions. Depending on their answers I might gather enough information to reach some conclusions."

Father Mark was almost speechless, but not enough to prevent him from saying, " Well that is very interesting Father Damian. I hope your research proves to be beneficial. I will mention to Father Charles that we have been speaking and I'm sure I will hear from Father John shortly. And when I do I will tell him you are waiting for his call."

"Thank you Father Mark it is always a pleasure speaking with you".

Father Mark hung up the phone. Looking pale and dumbfound he put his head down on his desk and groaned. "What in the world is going on? Am I dreaming? Am I insane? Three intelligent priests, one a seasoned orthodox theologian, and all are saying that animals speak. Before I call the psychiatrist I need to meet with Father Charles and Father John. I need to extend to them one last opportunity to recant this insanity. I can't let any of the priests or staff know about this. If any of the benefactors hear of it they will probably cancel their attendance at our annual barbeque this Saturday. And that's only six days away."

Father Mark pushed away from his desk and walked to the door. Before speaking with Father Charles he needed to know what Father John had discussed with Father Damian. Walking down the hallway he prayed silently for wisdom and patience. He sensed he needed both.

30

Cornered

Knowing that time was running out for Waldo, Target raced to the river, flying just above the tree tops. Although this was definitely more dangerous than flying through the trees he sensed that if an eagle or hawk did spot him he could fly into the dense underbrush close to the ground and escape his predators. Minutes later he approached the river and descended to ground level cruising just above the river bank. Remaining silent, he searched for Lightning as he closed in on the tree line, gliding quickly from tree to tree without flapping his wings. Suddenly, Lightning jumped out in front of him waving for him to stop.

"Lightning, I found Aroma, but he can't speak to the priests because the priests are banned from the valley. He wants you to go to the priests and tell them about Waldo."

"Impossible… I can't risk being killed; my kittens will starve to death."

"So what do you suggest?"

"Lead the way to Aroma. I need to convince him to go to the monastery and speak with the priests. Waldo will die if he doesn't."

"Let's go."

Target flew west, fifty feet above ground level, while Lightning raced directly behind him.
Target had little to contend with while flying, but Lightning had to constantly dodge fallen trees and large rocks which slowed him down.

"I can see the dirt path in the distance, we're getting close."

Out of breath Lightning called back, "Tell Aroma I'm right behind you so when he sees me he won't panic and think I'm going to hurt him."

Target made the turn and headed south to Aroma's tree house. Lightning reached the path and stopped to rest. After a minute he slowly started walking in the direction of Aroma's home, wanting to give Target a chance to explain that he was on the way. Half way there he saw a small cloud of dust quickly moving in his direction. Just above the cloud he saw Target flying towards him.

"Aroma is right behind me"

Suddenly the cloud stopped, and as the dust settled Aroma became visible, standing still, fifty feet away from Lightning who also had stopped. For a silent moment the two apprehensively stared at each other.

"It's ok Aroma. Don't worry, I won't hurt you. Waldo has been shot. He has lost much blood and needs water. He's too heavy for us to carry to the water so we will have to bring water to him. Only humans can do that."

"Lightening, I'll try to get the priests to bring him water and also a veterinarian, but I can't see them until nightfall."

"That will be too late. Waldo is still bleeding and will die if he doesn't have help soon."

Aroma seemed perplexed as he silently stared at Lightning. He knew it would be almost impossible to get inside the monastery in the day time, but even if he did he had no idea where Charlie or John would be.

"Make up your mind Aroma. We're wasting precious time."

"Ok, Ok... I'll try to get the priests attention, but it's a mile from here and I'm not a fast runner."

"Jump on my back. I'll get you there in two minutes"

Aroma was reluctant to jump on a bobcat's back that could suddenly change his mind and turn and kill him.

"Are you sure you won't hurt me?"

"You saved my life. I will never hurt you."

Aroma jumped onto Lightning's back, and Lightning took off like a rocket, racing through the woods faster than Aroma could ever have imagined.

"As soon as you see a clearing we need to stop".

In less than two minutes the clearing came into view and Lightning slowed to a walk as Aroma jumped to the ground. Searching the hide-a-way and seeing no one, Aroma charged up the pathway to the monastery. Reaching the top he waved to Lightning to follow him. Reluctant to venture near humans, Lightning slowly walked up the path to the top as Target settled on a tree branch above Aroma.

Aroma took a deep breath... "Ok, we're here, and now we have to figure out a way to contact the priests."

Lightning looked at Target and back at Aroma. "Neither one of us know the priests and neither one of us can take a chance at being killed. This is up to you Aroma."

Aroma remembered the outside garden grape trellis he had used to gain entrance to a window which later had been closed. Hoping someone had reopened it he dashed to the gate and went inside. At that very moment Father Michael was looking out of his office window and watched Aroma dash from the valley to the entrance of the outside Garden. Thinking it significant he rushed to tell Father Mark and met him at the main hallway as he was on his way to speak with Father John.

"Father Mark, I'm not sure what this means but I just saw a skunk rush from the valley to the outside garden. I wonder if Father Charles or Father John is meeting the skunk there."

Father Mark charged to the outside garden entrance at the end of the side hallway and burst through the door. Running to the center of the garden he searched in all directions and was stunned to see Aroma climbing the grape trellis and reaching for the window.

"Father Michael, quickly run inside and lock that window."

Father Mark bolted to the outside garden gate and locked it.

"Ok mister skunk, we have you locked inside. Now we'll see if you're the mystery skunk that Father Charles says can talk."

"I locked the window Father Mark."

"Thank you Father Michael. Now please have Father Charles and Father John report to me immediately."

Aroma was frantic. If he spoke to Father Mark

THE MONK & THE SKUNK

he might call an animal control officer and have him taken away. If he didn't speak then Father Mark might think he was just looking for food from the grapes and then let him go. But the thought of Waldo bleeding to death, and the urgency of getting him help, caused Aroma to blurt out… "Father Mark, I need your help. My friend Waldo has been shot and is bleeding to death."

Father Mark was stunned and felt faint as he fell back against a table of potted plants and landed on the floor just as Charlie walked through the door.

"Father Mark are you all right, let me help you up"

"That skunk spoke to me. I heard him. He spoke to me. I feel dizzy."

"Charlie, what's going on?"

"John I just got here but Father Mark heard Aroma speak and he sort of fainted and fell against this table and landed on the floor."

"I was trying to get into the building to find you Charlie. Waldo has been shot by a hunter and is bleeding to death. He desperately needs water but we animals can't bring it to him. We need your help."

"Where is he"?

"Very near the highway that leads into the high country. He's 50 feet inside the woods and lying on the ground. We can reach him by going through the valley and then crossing the river but we could save a lot of time by taking the highway."

"Do you know the exact spot?"

"No; but Target and Lightning do. They can travel with us and show us the way. "

"Who is Target and Lightning?"

"Target is a bird and Lightning is a bobcat."

Father Mark was overwhelmed and remained silent as he slowly stood up with the help of Father John.

"Tony the roofer is here with his truck Charlie. Maybe he'll agree to drive us and we can all try to pick Waldo up and take him to Dr. Dean the Veterinarian."

"Impossible John, he weighs 400 pounds. But maybe you can convince the veterinarian to drive in the truck with us and then he can help Waldo in the woods."

"Wait a minute. Slow down. No one is going anywhere without my permission. I'm not so sure any of this is real. And before I agree to inform the roofer that we need to save a wild boar who has been shot, plus tell him that we are taking with us a skunk, bird, and bobcat, all of whom can speak, I need to be sure we have not all lost our minds."

"You haven't Father Mark. Aroma can speak, I can speak, and Lightning can speak."

Father Mark's knees weakened once again as he stared in disbelief at a tiny bird perched on top of the garden wall.

"I didn't mean to scare you Father Mark. I'm Target. Lightning is outside. Trust me; you can believe everything you have heard. I know you're a bit overwhelmed at the moment but let me remind you that Waldo is bleeding to death. Every second counts and if we don't go to his aid, right now, he will die."

"Father John, Father Charles we need to pray. Please ask Father Michael to join us. We will need someone here at the monastery who knows where we are and what we are doing."

"I'm right here Father Mark. I was concerned for your safety with the skunk."

"Forget about that" Aroma insisted. "I never hurt anyone, including my fellow animals."

Father Mark composed himself and began to pray as Aroma bowed his head. "In the name of The Father, and of The Son, and of The Holy Spirit. Dear Lord Jesus, we are going to attempt to save a wild boar that has been shot. Please help us to be successful. If none of this is real and we are just hallucinating please let us know. Please give me the understanding that I need at this very unusual time. Thank you. Amen"

"Father Mark do you want me to speak with Tony or do you plan to?"

"Father Charles I would prefer that you speak with him because of your extensive knowledge regarding the animals speaking."

"John, do you want to come with me, I might need your testimony also."

"Sure Charlie. Father Michael, will you walk with Father Mark in case he's somewhat wobbly?"

"Thank you, but I'm ok now. Father Michael and I will get several water jugs for the trip."

Ten minutes later four priests and Tony loaded the truck with water and two large roofing tarps.

"Thank you Tony for helping us. I'm just as new to this animal speaking situation as you are. Half an hour ago I didn't believe it. Now, I have no choice. I'm told that you have been informed that three animals will be traveling with us; a skunk, a bird and a bobcat. Are you sure that this ok with you?"

"Father Mark, as long as they ride in the bed outside, that will be fine with me. But I don't want them in the front or back seat of the cab. And I don't mean to be rude, or jeopardize our business relationship, but are you all feeling ok? This is beyond strange."

"Sorry to put you through this Tony; yes we are feeling ok. Father Charles will you introduce Tony to the animals."

"Tony, this is Aroma. As you can see he is a skunk."

"How do you do Tony? Please rest assured that I will not spray you. I am a friendly skunk."

Tony nodded back at Aroma, not daring to speak lest he consider himself to be insane.

"Tony this is Target...

"Hold the phone gents. I do not ride in trucks. I'll fly back the way I came and meet you on the highway. When you get there I'll point out the spot where Waldo is."

"Oh! Ok... that will be fine Target. And finally Tony, Lightning..."

"Lightning isn't here Father Charlie. He's waiting for me back at the entrance to the valley. He can't risk being killed; he has small kittens to care for. He'll run to Waldo, while I fly ahead of him."

"Thank you, Target. I guess that means we're ready to go gentlemen."

Target flew to the Valley entrance to meet Lightning while Father Michael headed for his office.

THE MONK & THE SKUNK

Once Target had informed Lightning of the plans they abruptly disappeared from view and raced into the valley.

"Someone is going to have to pick me up and put me in the back of the truck. I would prefer that be you Charlie."

"Do you trust me Aroma?"

"Sort of... I have no choice really. Waldo is dying and we need to get moving."

As Tony pulled out of the driveway and headed for the mountain road, rescue plans unfolded. Once they found Waldo they would immediately stop the bleeding and give him as much water as he needed. Everyone agreed that they didn't have enough help to pick Waldo up and put him in the truck. The next best thing would be to roll him onto the two tarps and drag him to the shoulder of the road next to the truck. Once they had him alongside the truck they would pray that enough motorists would stop and offer help. If they were successful in loading Waldo into the truck they could immediately transport him to Dr. Dean. If no one stopped to offer help they would then bring the doctor to Waldo.

"We can drive to the area I think Target is talking about Tony and then just pull over and wait to see him signaling us."

"I know that area well Father Mark. I've seen the hunters parked alongside the road for many years. They usually leave their trucks on the shoulder and walk into the woods."

"That's great information Tony! It will give us a good indication where Waldo is. But we better not speak with any of them if they're out of the woods and standing by their trucks. They could be the ones who shot Waldo and might want to finish him off."

Several miles later the road grew steeper as the elevation increased. After ten minutes of climbing, the road started to level off again and they realized they had reached the high country. Reducing speed Tony advised his passengers to begin looking for any signs of Waldo.

"Look on the right side. Wild boar country is west of this road and east of the river."

Charlie was more anxious than anyone. He had personally counseled with Waldo and knew how devoted he was to his family. He also knew that Waldo and Aroma had been good friends, for many years, but had not yet reconciled. Looking over his shoulder and seeing that Aroma was safely huddled under the tarps, he quietly prayed, asking God to spare Waldo, at least long enough for him to reconcile with Aroma.

31

Tense Moments

Still wet from charging through the river, Lightning raced the last few feet to the top of the hill and settled down to rest. Exhausted, he searched the tree tops hoping to find Target. With the clearing a short distance away he would need Target to help him make a safe passage to the other side. Regaining his strength would take a few minutes, but then he needed to move quickly. Time was not on Waldo's side, and the clock was ticking. After several minutes of rest, and searching unsuccessfully for Target, Lightning became anxious and began to run toward the tall grass. Reaching the grass, and still no Target in sight, he charged ahead and continued running until he reached the clearing. Resting for a moment to catch his breath he planned to cross in the usual manner. Search the perimeter, especially the other side where he planned to go, and if no boars are in sight he would race at top speed until he was well into the woods. This was especially dangerous because a short distance into the woods there could be one or more boars who would attack him as he blindly charged into their midst.

"I have no choice. I need to help Waldo and I need to get home to my kittens. Where are you Target, you were just ahead of me at the river? I'll give you another minute and then I have to move"

Just as Lightning took a deep breath, and was about to make his risky charge to the other side, he spotted Target flying in his direction. Realizing that

Target didn't see him; he dashed a few feet into the clearing and signaled him. Target immediately swooped down and hovered just above Lightning.

"Wow, I'm glad I saw you. I thought you would still be down by the river. Waldo is fading fast. I don't think he is going to make it. I spoke with him but the priests and Aroma are not there yet. The hunters are all heading for their trucks. One truck is only 100 feet from Waldo but the hunters don't know he's there."

"What about the clearing, is it safe to cross?"

"Yes, all the boars are hiding from the hunters".

"Let's go. We can't let Waldo die alone. He needs to have someone with him. I'll start running and you check for danger ahead. I'll follow you."

Twenty minutes later Lightning had to rest, leaving only ten minutes between him and Waldo. Target flew ahead to see if the priests had arrived so he could show them the way to Waldo.

As he reached the highway he spotted Tony's truck heading north as if it were going back to the monastery. Alarmed that they may be leaving he raced to catch them and flew directly next to the driver's window. Tony slowed and pulled over as everyone rolled down their windows.

"Tony, you're going the wrong way."

"I know, we were just cruising back and forth waiting for your signal. There are a half dozen trucks with hunters back there. It looks as though they're getting ready to leave. There is another truck with no one in it not far from here. That hunter is probably still in the woods."

"He is, and he has another hunter with him.

THE MONK & THE SKUNK

Waldo is north of that truck by about 100 feet. I'll fly to the other side of the road and you can park right where I go into the woods. You better hurry, Waldo is very weak and needs water."

Tony crossed the highway and pulled onto the shoulder of the road. Charlie and John jumped out, grabbed water jugs, and followed Target into the woods. Father Mark and Tony started to follow when they heard, "Hey, put the tail gate down, this is too high for me to jump out." Turning they saw Aroma pointing toward the tail gate. As soon as Aroma hit the ground he raced into the woods followed by Tony and Father Mark.

"Father Charlie, he's over here behind these bushes", Target whispered from a tree branch. "Don't make a lot of noise, those other hunters must still be nearby. I'll fly around and look for them."

As Target flew off Charlie reached Waldo and silently knelt down next to him while John inspected his wounds. "He doesn't seem to be bleeding Charlie. The wound is caked in dried blood but there doesn't appear to be any fresh blood.

"Waldo, can you hear me? It's Father Charlie from the monastery. We came to help you."

Waldo struggled to lift his head and speak but his weakness caused him to put his head back down on the ground. "I need water" he pleaded barely above a whisper. As Charlie slowly poured water into the side of Waldo's mouth, Aroma arrived and stood next to Waldo. Noticing that his eyes were closed, he kept silent not wanting to disturb his drinking of the life saving water. Tony and Father Mark stared in amazement. For them, this was an unbelievable experience which they never would have imagined two hours earlier. As Waldo drank he occasionally coughed, causing Charlie to slow the volume he was dispensing. When the first gallon jug was empty Waldo seemed unable to continue. He needed to rest and regain his strength.

"I think he drank about half of that Charlie; the rest is on the ground."

"I know John, but I had to get as much in him as possible. We still have three more jugs we can give him when his strength returns."

"Waldo, it's me, Aroma. We're going to get you out of here."

Instantly Waldo opened his eyes and attempted to speak but could attain only a whisper.

"Aroma…Aroma I forgive you, I forgive you" he blurted out before drifting off into semi-consciousness.

Father Mark quietly announced that Target was flying in their direction. Landing on a tree branch he whispered, "two hunters are slowly moving in this direction. I don't know if they're going toward that truck nearest us or if they will continue in this direction. I'll keep you posted."

As Target flew off Aroma moved closer to Waldo. With tears in his eyes he quietly whispered, "Thank you for forgiving me my friend".

Father Mark grew anxious that hunters were approaching and suggested that the two tarps be brought immediately so Waldo could be pulled to the truck. Target continued searching the immediate area near Waldo. Suddenly he spotted Lightning running in his direction. Gliding to meet him he came to rest on a fallen tree.

"Target, how is Waldo?"

"He's weak but still alive. They just gave him some water. Be careful there are two hunters walking in this direction."

"Don't worry, I just passed them and they're walking towards the highway."

Target flew to the rescuers to inform them of the hunter's status. Lightning cautiously followed but remained out of sight as he didn't trust humans.

"The hunters are moving toward the highway. I'll fly out and see if they are the owners of that truck. Lightning is here but will probably remain hidden for safety's sake."

Aroma called to Target... "Wait! Tell lightning we need his help. Waldo is very heavy"

Target circled around and pleaded with Lightning to help pull Waldo to the truck.

"I don't trust them. I need to get home and protect my kittens."

"It's just for a few minutes. Don't worry they're safe. They really want to help Waldo."

Lightning reluctantly moved toward Waldo but still kept his distance. Father Mark spotted him hiding behind some thick vegetation. "Lightning, we need your help. None of us will hurt you. We are trying to save Waldo's life. Tony and Father Charlie are bringing the tarps so we can roll Waldo on top of them and then drag him to the truck. You can help us pull the tarps."

Lightning remained silent but slowly moved toward Waldo and stopped twenty five feet away.

"Father Mark we'll try the big one first. If it's not big enough we can tie the two together. I brought some rope from the truck"

"Thank you Tony. Once we get him to the truck we'll have to hope some motorists will stop and help us. He's much too heavy for the four of us to pickup."

Aroma explained to Waldo what was about to happen, but Waldo seemed to be unconscious. Once the big tarp was rolled out on the ground everyone positioned themselves next to Waldo. The plan was for each person to grab one of his legs and pull him onto the tarp. Then they would wrap the remaining portion around him and tie it off with rope. Father Mark gave last minute instructions…

"Ok, everyone grab a leg, and when I say 'go', pull him onto the tarp. Ready…GO!" Waldo squealed in pain as his right front leg was pulled by Charlie.

"Waldo we're sorry; we're just trying to help you", Aroma explained as he moved closer to comfort his wounded friend.

Tony released Waldo's left front leg and moved towards his head. "Father Mark you take my place by his left leg and I'll' pull from his head and neck. Moments later Waldo was safely on the tarp and John and Charlie tied the sides together. Fortunately only one tarp was needed.

"We're ready to go", Father Mark announced. "Lightning if you can grab the front of the tarp with your teeth, and the rest of us can grab a piece of the Rope, we can begin to pull Waldo to the truck.

Ready……Go"!

As Lightning walked backwards, pulling the tarp with his teeth, everyone else walked forward dragging 400 pound Waldo to the truck. Stopping only once to rest, they continued until they reached the truck. Aroma was very concerned for his safety and hid underneath the back of the truck. Leaning against the truck to catch their breath, they watched for cars and trucks going by in the hope of noticing someone who might help. Traffic was light with only an occasional car passing on their side of the highway. Suddenly Target flew towards them from the south.

"The two hunters are almost to the edge of the woods. It looks as though they're going to that truck just up the road."

Moments later they reached the truck, stowed their rifles, and pulled onto the highway. Driving south for only a few feet, they made a sudden u-turn and headed north. As they passed Tony's truck they stared at the tarp on the ground but continued north in the direction of the monastery.

"Father Mark, I worried for a moment they would notice Waldo and turn around."

"So did I Father Charles, but it seems we're in the clear for the moment."

Twenty minutes passed and only three cars had gone by. No one looked in their direction and none of them seemed as though they would be able to help.

"Father Mark you better try to reach Dr. Dean, Waldo needs help right away."

"You're right Aroma. Father John do you have your cell phone with you?"

"I do Father Mark."

"Please call Father Michael and tell him to call the veterinarian. Explain the situation and give him directions so Dr. Dean can find us."

Minutes later Father John's phone rang; "John, the Vet said he would be there in a half hour. He has a ramp you can attach to the truck. Then you can slide the boar into the back of the truck and transport him to the Vet's office."

Two hours later Waldo was receiving plasma intravenously in the back of Tony's pickup truck which was pulled into the Veterinarian's garage out of the sun.

"The bleeding was strictly from flesh and hide. The bullet entered the back of his shoulder and exited the front but never went deep enough to hit any major veins, or arteries, or bone. Because his shoulder is so thick and the bullet was spinning, the exit hole is the size of a quarter. That's why he had so much bleeding. I'm going to numb his shoulder and sew him up with a dozen or so sutures. He'll be very weak for several days. He has lost an immense amount of blood. Infection could become a problem so I placed some anti-biotic in the IV and it should do the trick. This was very kind of you to help this poor animal Father Mark. When I was driving up to meet you I passed a truck with a small dead boar in the back that had been killed by the hunters. They usually kill a dozen or so every season. You'll need to change the IV every four hours, until tomorrow. Then give him plenty of water and food for a week. I'll stop by and remove the sutures in 7 days."

"Thank you doctor" Charlie offered as Tony backed the truck out of the garage.

Driving back to the monastery, Father Mark instructed Charlie and John to set up the large tent they use for summer camping trips. The plan was to put Waldo inside and keep him safe until he healed. Space on the lawn outside the monastery was becoming limited because of the annual barbeque. Workmen had set up tables and chairs and a large covered area for the portable outside kitchen.

"Put the tent over by the Pieta. That will place Waldo about 100 feet from the kitchen and away from the guests. We don't want them seeing him. They'll never understand or believe any of this."

32

Stunned

Preparations were hurriedly underway for the Annual Barbecue. The monastery chef and several benefactors were preparing enough food for 100 guests and 27 monks. The catering truck had just departed after setting up the mobile kitchen with a large rotisserie grill on wheels, two large ice machines, a walk in refrigerator, and 3 mobile sinks. Most of the food had been supplied by the monastery with the remainder donated by the benefactors. Two hours from now, at 11 AM, the guests would arrive and the annual barbecue would begin. Five days earlier John and Charlie had set up the tent for Waldo's convalescence. With rest, and plenty of food, Waldo was recovering nicely, but still remained weak. He walked with a limp during the night hours in an effort to build up strength in his wounded shoulder. He never ventured out during the day time lest he be seen by those who were unaware of his presence. In two more days, early Monday morning, the veterinarian would arrive and remove his stitches.

"Charlie, I just received a phone call from Father Damian. He's coming to the barbeque and will arrive about 12:00. He said he has reached some conclusions he wants to share with us. "

"Good news John. We probably should get Father Mark in on the conversation also now that he knows the truth about the animals talking."

"I've already told him. He's anxious to hear what Father Damian has to say. By the way, he wants either you or me to give Waldo some last minute instructions about remaining out of sight while the guests are here. He doesn't want anyone frightened."

"I'll do it John. I planned to check on him anyway."

As Charlie walked toward Waldo's tent he noticed Father Mark arriving and making his way toward the kitchen. Making sure all the food was in place was a big undertaking and Father Mark didn't want any shortages.

"Good morning Father John, how's it going?"

"Very well Father. All of the salads are ready to go and waiting in the walk in. Most of the vegetables are cleaned and ready to boil. We'll begin that about 10:30. And the meat is going on the rotisserie right now and should be ready by noon."

"Excellent. I appreciate all your hard work. The baked pies and cakes are inside and we'll bring them out as soon as they're ready."

As Charlie approached Waldo's tent he whispered, "Waldo, it's me Charlie. I'm coming in." Waldo was resting on his left side making sure not to irritate his right shoulder.

"Father Mark wanted me to remind you that we will have more than 100 people here for the barbecue in a few hours, and he requests that you remain in the tent. If anyone sees you they might panic and run away, and the annual barbecue will be ruined."

"No problem Charlie. I'm still quite weak. I walk at night, but I'm not very fast. I imagine I will be limping for at least another month. That bullet did a lot of damage."

"You're welcome to remain here as long as you like Waldo. We're happy to provide you with all the help you need."

"There is one thing I could use Charlie but I don't know how you'll accomplish it. I need to get a message to my family and inform them that I'm ok and will be home as soon as possible."

"Wow, that's a tough one Waldo. I don't know where they live and even if I did that can be very dangerous country."

"Have you seen Target since you rescued me Monday in the high country"?

"No, but when you see Aroma tonight ask him if he can get word to your Family"

"I asked him last night, but he also mentioned the danger, and I had to agree with him. He was hoping that lightning would stop by but that's unrealistic. He never really goes past the river. My best chance is Target."

"That gives me something to pray about Waldo, and I'll do that tonight during prayer time."

During the next two hours the preparations continued and by 11 AM all was ready as the first guests began to arrive. By noon a few of the last to arrive made their way into the parking area along with Father Damian from the university.

"Welcome Father Damian, we're happy you could make it."

"Thank you Father Mark. I appreciate your invitation. It looks as though you have a good crowd here today."

"Yes we do. Allow me to show you around and

introduce you to some of our guests."

During the next hour, as the music played, Father John and Charlie encouraged the guests to approach the serving line and begin the feast. The chef picked up the microphone and informed the guest of the menu, listing one delicious dish after another.

"And finally ladies and gentlemen, the center piece of the banquet is a sumptuous young pig on the rotisserie, slowing turning to perfection. Just step up and we'll carve your individual selection."

Waldo slowly stood and limped to the tent entrance. He wasn't sure what the chef had said.

"John, did you know about the pig."

"No. Charlie. It's been roasting under the cover which they only just rolled back."

Two men approached the table with their plates filled with vegetables. The first one motioned to the chef... "I'll take a slice of that pig chef, I bagged that beauty five days ago in the high country. "

Waldo pushed through the entrance of the tent and slowly hobbled toward the kitchen. As he approached closer and closer he suddenly started charging towards the rotisserie.

"RANDY!!... RANDY!! You're cooking my nephew Randy. Leave him alone. Stop! Stop that machine. Take him off... leave him alone" Waldo pleaded as tears streamed down his face. Charlie rushed to Waldo as the guests ran towards the monastery for safety. Father Mark grabbed the microphone... "Don't be alarmed, he is harmless. He is recovering from a bullet wound and is upset that his nephew was killed. He is one of those animals that can talk just like humans."

Most of the guests were shocked and alarmed with about 50 making their way to the parking lot. Those remaining kept their distance from Waldo as Charlie tried to comfort him.

"Waldo I am so sorry. I knew nothing of this."

"Turn it off Charlie. Please turn it off. Take Randy off that spindle and put him in the tent with me."

As Charlie and the chef turned off the rotisserie, and began to remove Randy from the spindle, Waldo turned and looked at the crowd which was staring in disbelief. Trying to compose himself, amidst his tears and trembling, he gathered all his strength...

"You humans…, you say you love God. If you love God then you should love us animals like He does. But no… you don't love us. You kill us instead… and then you cook us."

Waldo lowered his head and sobbed. He was in pain, exhausted, and heartbroken. Slowly he began to limp towards the tent. The chef and Charlie had wrapped Randy in a large piece of plastic and were respectfully carrying him behind Waldo as he painfully made his way towards his temporary home.

Father Mark picked up the microphone and addressed the remaining guests and his 26 confreres.

"Please accept my apologies for this very unusual experience. I'm sure you are shocked to hear an animal speak. I was amazed myself, just a few days ago, when I actually had a conversation with a bird and a skunk. We were hoping to keep this a secret, but now, with the other guests gone, and probably telling all their friends, it looks as though we will have crowds venturing out here to the monastery on a regular basis."

Father Damian approached Father Mark, and the two discussed the next logical move.

"I've done some research about the animals and whether they have souls, and I'll be happy to share that with you when you have some time Father Mark. I think it would be smart to have everyone here at the monastery, on the same page. There will be much gossip, and much news coverage by the media."

"Are you free to celebrate Mass tomorrow morning Father Damian? You could use your homily time to share your insights with us. There is no retreat this weekend so it will only be the priests and brothers."

"Yes, I will be honored Father Mark. I'll see you about 7:30."

33

A New Ball Game

Aroma patiently waited for the late afternoon sun to settle in the west. He wanted to get to Waldo's tent but didn't want any of the remaining guests to notice him. Today had enough commotion without him adding to the upset. As the last guests made their way to the parking lot he dashed across the expansive lawn to Waldo's tent.

"Waldo, can you hear me; it's Aroma?

"I hear you."

"Is it safe for me to come in?"

"Yes"

As Aroma entered he looked toward Randy's body.

"That's Randy my nephew. The humans cooked him."

"I know, I watched the events of today but didn't want to add to the problems, so I stayed out of sight. How is your shoulder doing? That was a long walk to the kitchen and back."

"It still hurts when I stand, but if I lay down on my left side the pain goes away."

"Well, just continue to lie on your side and every night when you walk it will probably begin to get better. Waldo, I want to tell you something. Since you forgave me a few days ago I have been noticing that I don't feel guilty about so many things I have been feeling guilty about. I think it is because when I offended you, and you were so hurt that you couldn't bring yourself to forgive me, my sense of guilt stayed with me in all areas of my life. I was wrong to offend you, but when you refused to forgive me I felt somewhat unforgiveable...I guess. I'm not positive about this analysis but now that you have forgiven me I feel forgiven and my sense of guilt in general has greatly lessened. I feel as though I am acceptable again. Does that make sense to you?"

"It does. Just make sure you don't do it again."

"I won't Waldo, trust me."

"Aroma, I really need to get a message to my family. I want them to know that I'm safe. I also need to inform my brother Bob that Randy has been killed."

"As I mentioned to you before Waldo, the only way we can accomplish that is by having Target deliver the messages. He knows where everyone lives. His home is in the tree just above where you rested by the highway, but that is too far for me to travel. I heard Father Damian speaking with Father Mark and he is going to be giving a homily tomorrow morning and I'm going to listen. After Mass I'll try to get Father Charlie's attention and ask him to have someone drive to the spot and call Target. He'll probably answer if he recognizes who ever calls him. What are your plans for Randy?"

"I don't know. I was hoping to hear from Bob. He is his father and has the right to decide what to do with his body. Ask Father Charlie to have the person who speaks with Target to also ask him to inform Bob about Randy's body. We need to know what he wants us to do."

34

Searching for the Truth

The Sunday morning sunrise filled the monastery with light as 27 priests and brothers, followed by their guest celebrant, processed into the chapel. This was not the first time that Father Damian had been the celebrant. For the last fifteen years he had led a dozen or more retreats, especially those that highlighted the church's theology, dogma, and doctrine. When the entrance hymn concluded, Aroma positioned himself next to an open window near the front of the chapel. As Mass progressed he carefully listened to the Gospel reading. Immediately thereafter Father Damian would begin his homily and Aroma would hear what Charlie and John had been eager to hear since their meeting last week... 'What is the meaning of the word 'dominion' when used in the context of mankind having 'dominion' over the animals? As the last words of the Gospel echoed through the chapel Father Damian paused, and looked directly at his fellow priests and brothers.

"Today's homily will be somewhat instructive and somewhat speculative. I wish it weren't so but the questions we will explore have gone unanswered for centuries. And while I don't presume to have those answers I believe we do have the freedom to prayerfully speculate what those answers most likely would be.

The question that has been put to me; 'what did God mean when he gave humankind dominion over the animals', is a good question to consider, especially in light of the recent developments here at the monastery. My research and subsequent conclusions are what I wish to present to you today. I ask that you consider them as fact where I quote Holy Scripture, and speculation where I reach conclusions.

The word dominion means 'to have authority over or control'. We know that God is our creator and has dominion over all of creation. We experience His dominion over us in the way he treats us. God is love and He treats us with love. He treats the animals with love also. Holy Scripture tells us in the book of Genesis that after God created the animals "God saw how good it was." So dominion in the sense of mankind having dominion over the animals would logically mean to have authority over or to control, but in a loving way. In a practical sense an ox can help plow a field, a horse pull a wagon, a dog can protect you. Dominion does not mean to kill. But what about food you ask? What about it? Holy scripture tells us that God said to man "See, I give you every seed-bearing plant all over the earth and every tree that has seed-bearing fruit on it to be your food; and to all the animals of the land, all the birds of the air, and all the living creatures that crawl on the ground, I give all the green plants for food". But then we also read in scripture that when Noah emerged from the Ark, one thousand one hundred and fifty nine years later, God said to Noah and his sons, "Be fertile and multiply and fill the earth. Dread fear of you shall come upon all the animals of the earth and all the birds of the air, upon all the creatures that move about on the ground and all the fishes of the sea; into your power they are delivered. Every creature that is alive shall be yours to eat; I give them all to you as I did the green plants."

Maybe God gave the animals to Noah and his family for food because the earth had been flooded and was not as yet yielding a harvest. I believe if we have nothing else to eat and we would otherwise starve, then it would be permissible to kill animals for food. But for any other reason, such as sport, I believe it is sinful. After all, we have a choice. Eat the food that is available, vegetables and fruit, or kill an animal. Really, the significant question is 'what do we want'? Do we want to take an animal's life unnecessarily when there are other things to eat? But what about further on in Holy Scripture where Jesus tells the apostles to throw their net on the other side of the boat. When they did, they caught so many fish they could barely pull the net in. He even cooked fish for them on a fire at the shore. Could it be that food was scarce and fish was the staple that kept people alive? Yes, that could be, and in that case I believe it would be permissible. But in our modern society with our advanced methods of farming we have a choice. Finally, there is the question of offering holocausts or animal sacrifices to God which we read about in The Old Testament. These were meant as adoration of God. We also read in the Old Testament, in the book of Hosea, chapter 6, verse 6, "For it is love that I desire, not sacrifice, and knowledge of God rather than holocausts." And in The New Testament we read in the Gospel of Matthew, chapter 9, verse 13, "Go and learn the meaning of the words, 'I desire mercy, not sacrifice'."

THE MONK & THE SKUNK

Now, the next question to explore concerns the animals and their future. Do animals have souls? Do they have a future in Heaven? Do they love? As I mentioned earlier these are centuries old questions and to date no one has answered them. I'll attempt to give you my take on all of that. First of all, as we have mentioned, God is love. He made us in His image and likeness. He therefore made us in the image of love. We are commanded to love. When we receive God's love it resides in our soul and we share His love with others. When we die, if our soul is filled with love, we return to God and live forever in Heaven. Do animals have souls? Do they love? Do they go to Heaven? If they have a soul, and are receptive to God's love, then they would be capable of sharing God's love with one another. I believe that animals express love and give love. The only place they could get this love would be from God. And His love would logically reside in their souls. So if they love, they have a soul. If they have a soul then they have the chance to go to Heaven. Are there good animals and bad animals? I believe that like humans, animals can behave in a sinful way or they can behave in a loving way. And I believe they choose one or the other. I was speaking with a fellow priest about this and he too is a theologian. He said I was spending too much time trying to discern if animals go to Heaven. He said he had a better question. He asked me "why wouldn't the animals be in Heaven?"

If we have a concern for the animals and whether they go to Heaven or not, we can rest assured that God cares even more than we do. After all, they are

His creation and He has called His creation Good. If we love the animals, I guarantee that God loves them more than we do. We should trust Him. He knows what He is doing.

Regarding the current situation with Waldo and his nephew Randy; the very least we should do is have a respectful burial for the poor animal. And considering that other animals will want to attend we should consider the valley as the appropriate place. They will feel much more comfortable, and less threatened, in that environment.

My fellow priests and brothers, we need much prayer in the days ahead. These are stunning revelations about the animal kingdom. Who would ever have imagined that they could speak as we do?"

35

Incredible!

Father Mark tapped his spoon on the side of his coffee cup hoping to gain the attention of his fellow priests and brothers. The conversation about Waldo and the animals has consumed everyone's attention since Saturday, and now during Monday morning breakfast there seemed to be no stopping the speculation about future events.

"Attention! May I have your attention please? Gentlemen we need to complete our plans for addressing the situation with the animals. We have much to consider and we need some of you to step forward and volunteer for various duties. This is going to be a major undertaking and our behavior around the animals will be of the utmost importance. The slightest wrong move, word, or gesture could send them running into the woods and thereby ruin our historic meeting. As of this moment the plan is as follows:

Tony the roofing contractor has agreed to drive his truck to the high country today to try to locate Target, the talking bird, who knows where the wild boars live. Specifically, we need to get word to Waldo's family and inform them of his condition. We also will be inviting them to the funeral we are planning for Randy, the boar we cooked on Saturday. Target will then bring the sad news of Randy's death to his family and invite them to the funeral which will be Thursday morning. We need to give the animals' time to make the journey and then rest for a day or two. Next we need volunteers to dig a grave and make some sort of headstone to mark the spot where Randy will be buried in the Valley. We have no idea how many other animals will attend but we are preparing for at least 50. Tony will also ask Target to spread the word in case there are other animals that knew Randy and might like to attend. Aroma, the talking skunk, will screen the animals for us and let us know if any of them are dangerous and should be excluded. I haven't come up with any ideas about what to do if that situation occurs. And lastly we need to bring about thirty chairs to the valley for ourselves, Father Damian, Dr. Dean the Veterinarian, and Tony. Father Charles will sing the entrance hymn, Father Michael will read the first reading, I will read the Gospel and give a very brief homily, and it appears that Aroma intends to give the eulogy. Does anyone have any questions?"

"Father Mark, we had many phone calls yesterday, as you are aware, and most of those callers were from news organizations seeking information about the talking animals. Apparently those who attended the barbecue have spread the word. What are your plans for handling unannounced visitors? By Thursday we could have a steady stream of strangers roaming about the property. Should they find their way to the valley on Thursday, we could have a problem with the animals thinking they have to defend themselves and someone might get hurt."

"That is a very good question Father Michael. I have briefly considered that possibility and have decided that we need to close the main gate the night

THE MONK & THE SKUNK

before. Certainly we need to pray about this entire situation and keep foremost in our minds that we are dealing with wild animals. Although they can talk and communicate with us, they are still animals. And some of them have the ability to injure or even kill us. Between now and Thursday I ask all of you to pray constantly and inform me of any thoughts or suggestions you may have regarding any and all of this. God Bless you."

36

Apprehension

Uneasy anticipation gripped the religious community as last minute preparations were underway for today's 'first ever' animal funeral. Father Mark reviewed the schedule with those who would play an active role in the service.

"Father Charles you have chosen Amazing Grace as the entrance hymn. We will process down the path and take our seats. I, along with Father Michael, you, and Father Damian will be sitting in the first four seats of the front row. Once we are all in place and the entrance hymn concludes, I will address the gathering and welcome the animals. Next, Father Michael will read the account in the book of Genesis that speaks of God creating the animals. I will then read the Gospel and give a very brief homily, followed by Aroma who will give the eulogy for Randy. At the conclusion of his eulogy he will invite any animal who wishes to eulogize Randy to come forward. Apparently Target was successful in notifying Waldo's and Randy's families who have indicated they will be attending. He also reported that Lightning and his kittens, and many other animals, will also be here. All of the clergy will wear white albs and the brothers will wear their black cassocks."

Preparations continued throughout the morning as the appointed hour approached. At 10 AM sharp the bell tower rang and the procession from the outside garden to the valley began with Charlie playing his guitar and everyone else singing along. At the head of the procession was Aroma, followed by Charlie, Dr. Dean and Tony. Immediately behind them were the monks, and finally Father Michael, Father Damian, and Father Mark. Waiting in the Valley was an impressive array of animals. Out of suspicion and anticipation most were remaining in the woods very near the edge of the clearing. Waldo's family and Randy's family were in the middle of the clearing while Lighting and his kittens were perched on top of the boulder ready to jump to the safety of the woods if necessary. High up in the trees, Target kept watch; waiting to warn his fellow animals of the approaching humans. Slowly the procession reached the clearing and thirty humans began to take their seats, row by row, until all were present. Instinctively the animals stepped back, cautiously keeping their distance from potential danger. As the entrance hymn drew to a close Aroma smiled a fresh, new, happy smile as he recalled that he no longer considered himself to be a wretch as the hymn suggested. Thanks to Waldo's offering of those precious words "I forgive you", he was now able to forgive himself. As Charlie put his guitar down Father Mark stepped to the Pulpit.

"Good morning everyone, you are most welcome. We have assembled here today to pay our last respects to Randy who was killed 12 days ago during the hunting season. We give thanks to Almighty God for having created Randy and giving him to his loving family. And we ask your forgiveness for the hunter whose actions ended his young life. Hunting for animals, to kill them, is wrong when there is plenty of other types of food to eat. Because of this tragedy we have come to believe that reality."

As Father Mark continued with his brief introduction many of the animals emerged from the woods and stood in the clearing. His words denouncing the killing of animals eliminated some of their anxiety. Several of the monks became somewhat anxious as they gazed fifty feet away at skunks, bobcats, large boars, raccoons, opossums and fox. With the conclusion of his welcoming address Father Mark introduced Father Michael who stepped forward to the pulpit. Spontaneously, the animals retreated towards the woods, unsure once again for their safety.

"Good morning Animals. We are your friends. Please be a peace. I will now present to you a reading from the book of Genesis. 'Then God said, "Let the earth bring forth all kinds of living creatures: cattle, creeping things and wild animals of all kinds." 'And so it happened: God made all kinds of wild animals, all kinds of cattle, and all kinds of creeping things of the earth. Gods saw how good it was.' The word of the Lord."

Father Michael returned to his seat and Father Mark stepped to the pulpit to deliver the Gospel reading.

"To you my animal friends I offer this explanation. I will now deliver the Gospel reading taken from the Gospel of Luke, Chapter 6, verse 27 thru 36. These will be the words of Jesus as he spoke to his listeners. It is beneficial to dwell on His words as they help us in our daily lives. In the Gospel reading today we hear Him say: 'But to you who hear I say, love your enemies, do good to those who hate you, bless those who curse you, pray for those who mistreat you. To the person who strikes you on one cheek, offer the other one as well, and from the person who takes your cloak, do not withhold even your tunic. Give to everyone who asks of you, and from the one who takes what is yours do not demand it back. Do to others as you would have them do to you. For if you love those who love you, what credit is that to you? Even sinners love those who love them. And if you do good to those who do good to you, what credit is that to you? Even sinners do the same. If you lend money to those from whom you expect repayment, what credit is that to you? Even sinners lend to sinners, and get back the same amount. But rather love your enemies and do good to them, and lend expecting nothing back; then your reward will be great and you will be children of the Most High, for he himself is kind to the ungrateful and the wicked. Be merciful, just as also your Father is merciful.' The Gospel of Our Lord Jesus Christ.

Here we have a very interesting lesson given to us by Our Lord Jesus Christ. He is telling us to love one another. If for some reason we have been offended by some person or a fellow animal, we are to forgive them. We are to love our enemies and be merciful to them just as God is merciful to us. On behalf of the humans I ask for your forgiveness for the times we have offended you. And in particular to you Randy's family I offer my sincere apology for the senseless killing and cooking of your dear son and brother."

As Father Mark returned to his seat and Aroma approached the Pulpit, Charlie picked him up and placed him on top so he could be seen by everyone. Aroma looked out at his fellow animals and could clearly see Randy's mother visibly shaken with tears running down her face. By now the number of animals had increased to almost 100 with more seen in the woods approaching the clearing. Aroma moved close to the microphone.

"My friends, and I mean my animal and human friends, this is a very unusual situation. All of these humans here today have just recently learned that we can speak just like they can speak. They have also just learned that we can be happy and sad, angry and loving, frightened and brave. But most importantly of all, they have now learned that it is wrong to kill us."

Suddenly, Randy's father Bob moved towards Aroma and bellowed, "How could they have just learned it is wrong to kill us. We hear humans talking all the time and I have heard them quoting the Ten Commandments. They say 'you shall not kill.'

"They just mean humans shall not kill humans Bob. The commandments are not talking about us animals."

"Says who?"

"You're welcome to come forward Bob and ask any questions or make any comments you wish when you give your eulogy for Randy; but, please give me just a few minutes, I have something to say."

Bob nodded and returned to his wife's side. Only twenty five feet away, Randy's body, covered in canvas, waited for burial beside the grave prepared for him. At the head of the grave was a headstone with the inscription;

> Randy
> Killed by hunters
> While protecting his Family

After a brief pause Aroma began to speak.

"It is my understanding that Target has informed all of you animals that we are having a peaceful and friendly meeting here today to offer our respects to Randy and his family. He has also assured you that there is no threat or danger to you from the humans and that you are expected to extend the same courtesy to them. So please relax and take advantage of this rare opportunity to say whatever you wish to our human brothers and sisters. A week ago Thursday, Randy was shot and killed during the humans wild boar hunting season. That same day, Waldo was shot and wounded by another hunter. These humans, sitting right here next to me, saved his life. He is recovering in a tent at the top of the hill on the Monastery property. He wanted to be here today but he can't walk down the path with his wounded shoulder. When we are finished here, anyone who would like to visit Waldo is welcome to.

Randy was an animal who lived in the wild with all of us. He was our neighbor and friend. There was no good reason for anyone to interrupt or end his life; but, as we are aware, a misguided human killed him. Unfortunately, an equally misguided number of humans then choose to cook Randy so they could consume him. I know that some of you are still not vegetarians. You still kill your fellow animals and eat them. That is unnecessary. We have an abundance of vegetation to consume and I recommend that you seriously consider changing your diet in the near future. I have recently discovered, through the help of Father Charlie, that God really does exist and has actually created all of us. He is the humans God and our God. My understanding is that he loves us and wants us to love one another. He also wants us to forgive one another as He forgives us. So I ask you today to please forgive the humans for the horrible crime of killing Randy. Now, if anyone would like to speak, you are welcome to come forward. Bob, you were speaking before, would you like to continue?"

Bob was emotionally overcome and unable to compose himself, so his wife stepped forward and slowly walked to Randy's grave.

"Is this what I'm supposed to forgive? My son is dead and his body cooked and you say I'm supposed to forgive. Have any of you humans had your children killed and their bodies cooked. We are animals and we are vegetarians. We believe it is wrong to kill. But you, with all your access to fruit and vegetables still choose to unnecessarily kill us animals for food. And then you have a party to cook us. You are gluttons. You are murderers. You have torn our family apart. You do this every year. Stop killing us!!

An obvious sense of uneasiness crept through the ranks of the thirty humans sitting in the chairs. Shifting in their seats, they anxiously watched Randy's distraught mother walk back to Bob, as she too was now emotionally overcome.

"Please my fellow animals, realize that Randy's

THE MONK & THE SKUNK

mother is justifiably upset. My sense of things is that in time she will be able to forgive the humans. And we too must keep in our minds and hearts that forgiveness is necessary for our peace and happiness. Waldo has recently forgiven me and because of it I have experienced peace and happiness. His lack of forgiveness made me feel guilty all the time and it followed me into many areas of my life. I would feel guilty about things and situations that I had no real reason to feel guilty about. We must forgive one another. Forgiveness brings healing and peace to the forgiver and to the one who is forgiven. Now, would anyone else like to speak before we place Randy's body in the grave?

"Yes! I have something to say."

"Please, come forward Lightning."

"I'm more comfortable right here on the boulder protecting my kittens."

"That's fine. For those of you who don't know Lightning, he lives in the high country with his three kittens. His wife was killed by wolves a month ago. Go ahead Lightning"

"We have been listening to one another complain about the violence the humans perpetrate on us. But that violence doesn't come close to the immense violence we do to each other every day.

Until a few weeks ago, I killed daily to feed my family. And by doing so I was teaching my kittens to do the same thing. But since Aroma saved my life in the river I have been a vegetarian. I always felt guilty about the killing, but now I'm free of that. I strongly recommend to you, my fellow animals, that you stop the senseless killing."

"Thank you Lightning."

As Charlie placed Aroma on the ground, Father Mark stepped to the pulpit.

"At this time I ask that Randy's Family and friends please gather around Randy's body and we will begin his burial."

About twenty five animals approached Randy's grave while Father Mark read the appropriate prayers for the occasion. After singing several hymns the burial began. An unusual silence came over the animals. They had never witnessed one of their own being buried by humans. At the conclusion of the ceremony Father Mark addressed the very sad animals.

"Thank you all for attending this solemn funeral for Randy. I invite those of you who wish to visit with Waldo to please follow us up the path to the monastery."

Row by row the monks filed out and began the climb to the monastery. Following closely behind was Waldo's family and twenty or so other animals. Several other birds had joined Target and flew ahead to alert Waldo of the approaching visitors.

"Hey, Waldo, it's me Target. There's a bunch of your friends on the way to visit with you. Your family is also here and they will be the first to arrive."

Waldo burst out of the tent and looked toward the outside garden, hoping to see his family as they emerged from the valley. Slowly the monks appeared followed by Aroma, Lightning, and his kittens. Suddenly Waldo's wife and their two sons reached the top of the pathway and began walking toward the tent. Waldo ran as fast as his limping would allow. Spotting him, his two sons raced to his side.

"Dad, are you all right?"

Speechless, Waldo embraced his wife as the two tearfully hugged in silence. One by one his friends approached and shared their love and concern for this brave father who saved his family and almost died in the process. While the visiting continued Aroma introduced Charlie to each animal. As they roamed about the monastery property they eventually gathered around the Pieta and presented many questions to Charlie and John. Target shared his heartbreak over his lost baby bird with Charlie and asked if he had ever given counseling to birds. Several other animals approached Charlie and John and asked similar questions.

"May I have your attention please? Many of you have expressed an interest in counseling. Father John and I have discussed this and we are willing to counsel with any of you who wish to do so. Considering your collective interest in the Pieta, it seems as though this would be a good location for counseling. If you will please give us your name and the day and time that you would prefer for counseling, we will be happy to accommodate you. We can begin as early as tomorrow. For the sake of privacy I will counsel only one animal at a time, and Father John has agreed to do the same. We will be able to accommodate four in the morning and four in the afternoon for a total of eight per day. If you don't feel comfortable with either me or Father John, we have many other priests available to assist you."

By the end of the day, with the last animal departing for the valley, 18 had signed up for counseling. The only potential roadblock would be the increasing interest by the news media. The main gate would be unlocked by tomorrow.

37

Swamped

Father Mark fielded call after call from curious citizens and the media. He had developed a stock answer which he skillfully presented to everyone.

"Thank you for calling about this unusual situation. We are in the process of investigating this phenomenon and will have more detailed information for you as it develops. Please call back next week." With this being Friday morning, and no retreat scheduled for the weekend, Charlie and John would have three days to counsel the animals without interruption from outsiders. But what to do after that time was the question Father Mark chose not to address. And the thought of media reporters arriving unannounced was causing him considerable anxiety. As he left his office the phone rang again, prompting him to run back in and switch on the recording machine. Fortunately he had recorded his message earlier in the day and now everyone who called in would hear his request to call back next week. Curious as to how the counseling was going he walked to the outside garden to see if he could help in anyway. The counseling sessions went from 10 AM to 11 AM and from 11 AM to 12 noon. Then in the afternoon they would go from 1 PM to 2 PM and 2 PM until 3 PM. Now, at 10:30, the first session would be in progress. Walking through the outside garden gate he had a clear view of the sitting area next to the Pieta. At one end, sitting on a bench, he could see Father

Charlie counseling Target. At the other end of the area, about 100 feet away, he could see Father John sitting on a bench counseling Bob, Randy's father. During a meeting with the entire community immediately after breakfast the consensus was that all counseling would be treated with confidentiality, similar to the seal of confession. That way each animal would be confident that everything would be kept completely secret and never revealed to any animal or human. As Father Charlie continued speaking with Target, Father Mark decided that he didn't want to be seen and returned to his office.

"Target, have you tried to explain to your wife why pushing the third egg out of the nest was wrong?"

"I told her I would have made a bigger nest if I had known that she was going to kill our baby. Plus she saw how upset I was. I don't know what else I could have said. "

"Killing the unborn baby was wrong because all of God's creation is sacred. It is His, and He gives it all to us to love and to respect. For humans, the fifth commandment is 'thou shall not kill'. I'm beginning to think that that commandment also applies to animals in their own lives. Even though you can't read, you know instinctively that killing is wrong. If you could relay that information to your wife it might make a difference. She needs to be educated about God and the sanctity of life. I believe all animals need this education. Maybe we can develop a seminar in the valley, once a month, and teach you about God and creation and our responsibilities as stewards of all that He has given us."

"I'll bet I could drum up a lot of interest for that Father Charlie. In addition to my wife, the first bird I will bring with me is my neighbor. When I returned home, after the barbecue, he was trying to convince his wife to do the same thing my wife did. He said he had seen her push the egg out of the nest. He and his wife have two eggs and he wanted to push both of them out of the nest. His wife was hysterical and pleaded with him to keep the eggs. I flew over there and we got into a terrible argument. He said they already had given birth to three sets of babies over the years and he didn't want the responsibility any longer. He eventually listened to me but I had to leave shortly after that and I don't know if he changed his mind.. He's here today so I'll ask him after we finish talking."

"Target, when you return home, make a serious effort to forgive your wife. I know you told her you will never forgive her, but that was your emotion speaking at the time. God tells us to be forgiving and merciful just as He is forgiving and merciful. Surely, by now she will be feeling guilty. She is a mother and has gone against her natural instinct to protect her babies. She probably had reasons she never shared with you. Maybe she is like your neighbor and was tired of raising babies. But whatever the reasons, killing the babies is always wrong. Let me know how the situation develops the next time we counsel. For now it is almost 11 AM and our session is finished. I have another animal to counsel in a few minutes."

As Target left he headed toward Waldo's tent.

His family would be spending the weekend with him and would then return home Monday morning. At the moment they were touring the very large Monastery property and Waldo was free to accept visitors. Randy's father Bob was also just finishing up counseling and was slowly walking toward Waldo's tent.

"Waldo, it's me Target. Bob and I wanted to stop and say hello."

"Come on in, there's plenty of room."

"Hey Bob, …Target… how did your counseling go?"

"Waldo, Father John told me I needed to forgive the hunter who killed my son Randy. I told him I didn't think I could do that. He also told me I should forgive the people who cooked Randy. He said he knew how difficult that would be, but nevertheless I needed to forgive. We were a peaceful family and now our family is devastated. I don't know if we will ever be peaceful again. How can I forgive some human who killed my son and others who cooked him?"

"If you want to be peaceful again you better listen to Father John. I went for a month not forgiving Aroma and believe me I had absolutely no peace. It was awful. I was always agitated and restless. Once I forgave him my peace returned and Aroma had the same reaction. Forgiveness heals and renews both the forgiver and the forgiven. Trust me. It works."

"I'll think about it"

"Pray about it"

"What does that mean?"

"It means ask God to help you."

"I heard about God at the funeral yesterday but I know nothing about praying."

"I'll teach you after I speak with Target."

By 3 PM the counseling sessions were over and Waldo approached Father Charlie.

"Father Charlie, I know the counseling is finished for today, but do you have just five minutes?"

"Sure Waldo. How can I help you?"

"I understand the necessity of forgiveness, and I'm telling others about that, but why does God allow the hunters to kill us in the first place?"

"Waldo, God has given all of us free will. That means we can either choose to do his will or choose to do our own will. God loves each of us, including the hunter. If a hunter chooses to kill you for sport, God doesn't stop him. But that hunter is going against God's will. You told me during one of our conversations a few days ago that you weren't always a vegetarian. You said that you used to kill other animals for food when you could easily have had the green plants for food. . God let you do that. He longs for a change in all of us but He is patient and doesn't interfere with our free will. There is much more to this, and in the near future we will have teaching seminars in the valley for any animal who wishes to attend. Bring your friends."

38

Misguided

Several weeks of counseling had passed and the popularity of the sessions had caused additional hours to be added to the schedule. Father Mark and Father Michael were now counseling the animals also and Father Gabriel would be starting in a few days. Fortunately, Father Mark was able to convince the media to back off, telling them that none of the animals were willing to talk to the media, and if the media were to make a surprise visit, the animals would just run into the woods. All of that was true, and for now his request to the media to call for permission first, before visiting, was working.

"Charlie, with the additional hours of counseling, I think in a few weeks it will start to slow down. Many of the animals are content with two or three visits and then seem to be able to assimilate the suggestions into their daily lives. A few require longer counseling, but in time I believe our regular sessions will end. Then we can offer counseling on an appointment basis."

"I agree John. Also we have the first seminar in the valley in two days and I think that will give us an idea of what to expect in the future."

As John and Charlie were talking, the first client of the day was arriving from the valley. Accompanied by her parents, the young fox walked directly toward Charlie's bench as Father John departed and went to his counseling area.

"Good morning Father Charlie, I'm Cindy and these

THE MONK & THE SKUNK

are my parents. They brought me here today because They think I have a problem. I don't agree with them but they insisted that I speak with you."

"Good morning Cindy and Mr. and Mrs. Fox."

"Good morning Father Charlie. We don't really have last names. I'm Larry and this is my wife Marcia."

"It's a pleasure meeting you Marcia and Larry. I can counsel with Cindy alone or with all of you present, which ever you prefer. I do recommend however that I meet with Cindy first and then if need be we can all meet together."

"Actually Father Charlie we don't really need to meet with you. Cindy is aware of our reason for seeking counseling for her and she can discuss it with you by herself. We have had open discussions with her and she is very straight forward. She doesn't mind that we mention to you that she has a female friend and that she wants to marry her. We have told her that she needs a male friend, not a female friend, if she wants to get married. She disagrees and so we are here today."

"I see… well… ok. If you and Marcia would like to take a tour of our Monastery property I will spend an hour with Cindy and we'll see where we go from there."

As Marcia and Larry walked away Charlie prayed a beginning prayer for the session. "Dear Jesus, Our Savior, nothing is beyond your understanding. You know all things and reveal everything necessary for our salvation. Please tell us where to go with our conversation so the best for Cindy and her family will come about. Thank you. Amen"

"Whose is Jesus?"

"Jesus is God the Son, Cindy. He came from Heaven to save us from our sins."

"You're talking about human stuff, and I don't know anything about that. The reason I'm here is because my parents don't want me to see my friend any longer. I want to marry her because we are in love and my mom and dad just don't seem to get it."

"What do you mean when you say you are in love?"

"I mean I am very attracted to her. She is beautiful and very affectionate. We plan on having a family and spending our lives together."

"Because you are a female you need a male, not a female, if you want to raise a family."

"Not true. We can adopt babies."

"Let's go back to the love part. You say you love her because she is beautiful and affectionate. What would happen in ten years if she is no longer beautiful because she is old looking?"

"I'll probably be old looking too. But, she will always be affectionate."

"Suppose she isn't?"

"It sounds like your just trying to break us up."

"Cindy, I'm trying to protect you from a very sad future. Let's change direction for a minute. How is your relationship with your mom"?

"What relationship? She never talks to me."

"Is she affectionate?"

"No way, she just bosses me around."

"Does she love you?"

"I wouldn't know. She never said so."

"Does your dad love you?"

"Yes. He's awesome."

"Did you ever have a male friend?"

"Once."

"What happened"?

"He always tried to have sex with me, but because I always said no he left me for someone else. That's when I met Emma. She already liked females and she knew that affection would make me happy. She talked with me like my mom didn't. She was affectionate toward me like my mom wasn't. And she didn't try to have sex with me like my male friend always did. And she didn't leave me."

"What did you mean when you said that she already liked females?"

"Well, she had already had a relationship with another female but they broke up."

"How long have you been in a relationship with her?"

"Two years"

"Is everything the same now as it was in the beginning?"

"Pretty much, I guess".

"Is there anything different?"

"Well, yeah. But it's no big deal... I guess... I just hadn't expected it."

"Do you want to tell me about it?"

Cindy looked away from Charlie and seemed to wipe a tear from her eye. She started to answer and lost her voice.

"Is it ok with you if I try to fill in the gaps?"

Cindy nodded her approval and looked at the

ground.

"Has she asked you to have sex with her?"

Cindy nodded yes.

"Have you had sex with her?"

Cindy burst into tears and put her paws over her ears.

"Cindy, God loves you, and so do your parents. Your mom might have problems from her own childhood and finds it too difficult to give affection. But the affection you are getting from Emma isn't affection at all. She is just using you to satisfy her own lustful cravings."

Cindy pulled her paws away from her ears and shouted, "It's sick. It's just so sick! She acts like she is a male but she isn't. I hate it. I can't stand it. I just want to turn the world backwards like this never happened." Sobbing, Cindy pleaded, 'Father Charlie, please say one of those prayers for me, I hate myself. My heart is so very sad."

"Charlie placed his hand on Cindy's small head and prayed...Dear Jesus, please give comfort to Cindy, this burden is crushing her. And please help Emma. No one can be happy with this nightmare in their life."

As Charlie and Cindy sat in the silence, a quiet peace came over them. By the end of the session Cindy was beginning to smile as Charlie carefully outlined a wisdom filled plan for her future well being.

39

Blessed are the Merciful

Father Mark closed his office door and headed for the board room where he had scheduled a special meeting of the speakers for the first seminar in the valley. Because of their extensive experience with the animals, John and Charlie were included along with Father Michael and Father Gabriel who had spent many hours counseling the animals. Father Damian was also invited to attend because he would be the best person to field the many theological questions put forth by the animals.

"Good afternoon gentlemen. We have much to discuss today. According to our best estimates we will have at least 150 animals attending this first seminar. The latest information, which comes to us from Target, is that 50 to 60 of those animals will be birds. Before we discuss the topics to be covered, and who will actually address those topics, I have some unusual news to share with you. I received a call last evening from the man who actually shot Randy. He was at the barbecue, as you are aware, and witnessed Waldo's outrage at his nephew being cooked. Apparently, for the past two weeks, this hunter has suffered extreme guilt and remorse over his killing Randy and wants to apologize. He was hoping that I could arrange a meeting with Randy's family. I informed him of the seminar tomorrow morning and invited him to attend. He readily accepted and will be here at 9 AM.

That being said, we can now turn our attention to tomorrow's schedule of speakers. When we're finished with that, we should spend some time in prayer. We have a serious responsibility to explain our Faith accurately to the animals."

....

    By 8:30 AM the sun had advanced above the hill top and began to fully illuminate the valley. Standing at the pulpit to test the P.A. system, Father Mark could see in the distant woods a steady stream of animals making their way through the valley. Already the trees were filled with every imaginable type of bird. Waldo had made it successfully down the path and was near the flat boulder with his family who had made the trip from the high country with Bob and his family. It was always safer to travel in numbers. Aroma was running about greeting all the animals many of whom he did not know. As the hide-a-way was filling up fast he sensed a need to address the animals and give them instructions for places to sit and stand.

    "May I please have your attention? We will be starting in a few minutes and I would like to suggest that the bigger and taller animals sit or stand in the back by the edge of the woods, and the smaller animals move toward the front. That way everyone will have the opportunity to see the speakers and also be heard themselves."

    As Aroma continued to greet the animals, Fathers Charlie, John, Michael, Gabriel, and Damian arrived and began to take their seats. The decision had been made to keep the number of humans to a minimum lest the animals feel uncomfortable. Father Mark returned to the monastery to meet the hunter, and, to bring him to the valley. As the bell tower began to ring 9 AM, Father Mark and the hunter made their way down the path to the valley, arriving just as the last chime rang. As the hunter took the seat reserved for him he placed a guitar case on the ground next to his chair. Waldo immediately recognized him as the man who had said that he had bagged Randy. Leaning toward his wife, he whispered, "That's the guy who killed Randy." Bob heard him and began to fume. He turned to his wife and repeated over and over what Waldo had said.

"Ok, ok, I hear you Bob. Calm down this is supposed to be a friendly discussion about God and humans and animals. Please just calm down. Your anger won't bring our son Randy back."

"Good morning my friends, it is good to see you all back here again. I'm Father Mark for those of you who are here for the first time. This morning we are beginning our "Seminars in the Valley Discussion Series" and all of you are most welcome to attend our once a month discussions. After our speakers present their teachings to you, Father Damian will take your questions and give you the church's position as an answer. Then, you may present a follow up question to him if you have one. Our first speaker will be Father John who will discuss the necessity of forgiveness and mercy in our lives. Next, Father Gabriel will present the Ten Commandments, discussing in particular the fourth commandment, 'Honor thy Father and Thy Mother'. Our third speaker will be Father Michael who will discuss chastity. And our last speaker will be Father Charles who will discuss the sanctity of life. Please welcome Father John."

Father John walked to the pulpit amidst a strange silence. The animals were not accustomed to applauding and simply extended curious stares as he unfolded his prepared speech.

"Thank you Father Mark, and welcome to you my animal friends. Today I will discuss the necessity of forgiveness in our lives. By that I mean the forgiveness we need to extend to everyone who has offended us in anyway. As I look out, I see among you a family who has been tremendously offended in recent times. Even under those trying circumstances forgiveness is still the answer that Almighty God demands of us."

As Father John continued, Bob was becoming extremely agitated and restless as he continued to stare at the hunter who killed his son.

"Today we have an opportunity to put our desire to forgive in action. As you all know, Randy's funeral was just two weeks ago and his grave is to my left near the edge of the woods. We received an unusual phone call two days ago from the man who identified himself as the hunter who shot Randy. He asked if we could set up a meeting with Randy's family so he could apologize. We said yes, and invited him here today. He has requested that we use only his first name. Please welcome Kenney."

Once again, the silence preceded the speaker to the pulpit.

"Good morning. My name is Kenneth. My friends

call me Kenney. I have not been able to get more than a few hours sleep in the past two weeks since the barbeque. I have been haunted by the reality that I killed someone's son and I ..."

Kenney began to lose his voice as tears welled up in his eyes. Bob, still agitated, became even more so and began to slowly move toward the pulpit.

"As a result, I came to realize that I would never have peace until I apologized to Randy's family and made amends in some way. So today, to prove my sorrow and make amends to his family, I brought with me ...," Kenny paused and picked up his case and began to open it as Bob moved closer. Reaching into the case he began to speak again, "I brought with me the gun I used"... as he pulled out the gun and held it in the air chaos erupted as over 150 animals and 75 birds scattered in wild panic. Bob charged the pulpit, knocking it over, and lunged at Kenney pinning him to the ground. As he opened his mouth to bite, and possibly kill him, Waldo screamed, "NO BOB !! STOP!! WAIT!!... Kenney, why did you bring the gun?"

Kenney was trembling and terrified, afraid to even speak.

"Bob, back off. Just give him a chance to explain. It's ok Kenney, I won't hurt you. Go ahead and tell us why you brought the gun."

"I just wanted to tell him that I had taken the trigger and hammer out of the gun and that I wanted to bury it near Randy's grave and beg the family to forgive me."

Kenney began to tremble and sob uncontrollably as Bob backed off and Father Charlie moved in to help

Kenny to his feet. Randy's mother moved close to Kenney, and in a voice barely above a whisper said with tears in her eyes, "I forgive you Kenney. Don't be afraid, my husband won't hurt you. He's not like that. He is just lost without Randy. He has been sad and heart sick beyond description. I have never seen him like this. But, don't worry, he has never killed, not even for food. He wouldn't even bite you."

"Please forgive me Bob. Please forgive me, I never thought of you as a person. But I now see that animals are just like us. I will never kill an animal again."

Father Mark and Father John picked up the pulpit and waited before trying to restart the seminar. Bob had still not forgiven Kenney. Waldo took Bob aside and quietly explained Kenney's sincerity and the need for Bob to find peace. "Remember what Father John told you? You won't find peace until you forgive. That's good advice, and now is the time. This guy is for real. Let him bury the gun and you can bury your anger at the same time. Come on Bob...you can do it."

"Tell him to bury the gun first and then I'll try to forgive him."

Aroma called the animals back to the valley. Slowly, and cautiously, they returned one at a time. Father Mark stepped to the microphone, "In the spirit of mercy and forgiveness, Bob is going to try to forgive Kenney for killing his son Randy. Kenney is going to bury the gun directly next to Randy's grave, and he has promised to never hunt again. He is truly remorseful and has repented. Please, let us have silence as this expression of sorrow, and the gift of forgiveness, takes place."

As Kenney walked with the gun to the grave prepared for it by the monastery staff, many of the animals shed tears of sadness for Randy's family. Many too, exhibited looks of kindness toward Kenney who obviously was suffering as much as Bob. The moment Kenney reached the grave, and threw the gun into the earth, cheers of joy burst forth from the immense gathering of animals and birds. Bob walked to Kenney's side and said "I forgive you brother. And I know you are my brother because Father John said so. Turning to walk back to his family Bob hung his head as tears of joy ran down his face. Kenney expressed a tremendous sigh of relief. He would sleep tonight for the first time in two weeks.

Father Mark stepped to the microphone once again.

"Because of the unexpected confusion we have just experienced, and the obvious need for many of you to have your questions answered, I will ask Father Damian to step to the microphone. You may address your questions to him. Is there anyone who would like to present the first question?

"Yes, I have a question", answered a bird high up in one of the surrounding trees.

"Good morning, I'm Father Damian. How may I help you?"

"My name is Cynthia. I am a young adult and not married. Two months ago I was raped. Now I have an egg in my nest and almost everyone I know is telling me to push the egg out of the nest and kill the baby.

They say it is the baby of a rapist. I don't know what to do. First I suffered the trauma of being raped, and now my friends want me to become a murderer. It's easy for them to say the things they say, but they don't have to kill the baby, I do. It is difficult enough to live with the memory of the rape let alone adding to it the guilt of killing the baby. And I will have to live with the memory of being a killer the rest of my life. Even though it is the rapist baby, it is also my baby. I have a friend sitting on the egg right now. She takes turns with me every day. She is the only one who is telling me to keep the baby. I need your advice."

"Keep the baby. God is the creator of all life and wants us to respect all life. He understands your difficulty. But think of the happy future you will have teaching your little baby bird how to fly."

"Father Damian, may I interrupt and make a suggestion?"

"Sure Aroma, Go ahead."

"My fellow animals, I can't help but think that most of you agree with Father Damian. By a voice vote, how many of you think the baby bird should be killed?"

Very few voices emanated from the immense gathering.

"How many of you think your sister should keep the baby bird and allow it to hatch and live its life."

The entire woods and trees exploded in cheers of support for the young bird to keep her baby."

"There you have your answer sister. Most of us animals know right from wrong".

As Aroma walked away from the pulpit Father

Damian continued to answer many questions that were posed by the animals. When the final questions were presented and answered, the remaining speakers concluded the seminar. Before the animals departed, plans for the next seminar were outlined and the date set. Judging by the positive conversation of the animals, it promised to be even bigger than today's gathering.

40

Do animals go to Heaven?

Father Damian finished reading the Gospel and reached for his notes. Today's homily would be lengthy. The chapel was filled with retreatants and monastery staff waiting to hear his conclusions after having preached to the animals during three separate seminars. Since the last seminar, held almost a month ago, the animals have roamed freely about the monastery grounds and frequently gather around the Pieta which they refer to as "Jesus God". Because Father Mark instituted a policy of keeping the main gate shut at all times, unannounced visitors and the media have not been a problem. As a result the animals have come out of the woods on a daily basis to socialize with the priests and brothers. On one occasion, during a weekend retreat, the animals gave permission to Father Mark to allow the retreatants to meet them. Today that group has returned and is attending Mass in the chapel at the invitation of Father Mark.

Father Damian began to speak... "We hear in today's reading Eli instructing Samuel to answer God by saying, 'speak Lord for your servant is listening'. I wonder how many of us pray that way. It would certainly profit us to do so. But I'm afraid that in spite of all our good intentions, we're more likely to pray: 'Listen Lord, for your servant is speaking'. If we're honest, we have to admit we spend a lot more time bending God's ear than allowing him to whisper into ours.

THE MONK & THE SKUNK

Prayer is a conversation – and conversation is interactive. Once we have put our petitions before the Lord, we should allow an equal amount of time for quiet reflection – listening for that still, small voice that Elijah once heard. Jesus himself did that as we hear from our gospel reading: 'Rising very early before dawn, he left and went off to a deserted place where he prayed'. So often in Mark's gospel we read of Jesus being hemmed in by people who want something from him. Even today we read: 'The whole town was gathered at the door'. Jesus took care of their needs, but after healing them, he went off to the desert to pray.

This is a dynamic that will often be repeated in the gospel – Jesus ministry is fueled and refreshed by prayer. If Jesus himself needed a quiet time and place to hear the voice of God, how much more do we?

I mention this because so many of us have been searching for answers regarding the animals, and our prayers have been intense and constant. But are we listening to what God is telling us. Frequently the answers don't come as words in our ears but in circumstances he places in our lives.

Lately our questions have been many. Do animals love? Do they have souls? Do they go to Heaven? I even had someone ask me if animals sin, and, if they do, does God forgive them? That question alone brings me to the heart of my theology which is... "God is love, and Jesus loves to forgive."

During these past few months of counseling the animals have certainly revealed to us that they have the same strengths and weaknesses that we have.

And we are not the only ones asking these questions. Many of the animals have asked me if they can go to Heaven. So far I have told them 'I don't know.' But I also know that I have to wait and listen to the quiet voice of God for the answer. After these extremely interesting weeks and months I have come to conclude that I don't see why all of God's creation won't be in Heaven. It is all good and created by his hands. God loves us and he loves the animals. We love the animals and they love us. St Francis of Assisi had a very active love for the animals and all of God's creation. He is quoted as saying 'brother sun, sister moon'.

I will conclude with one final thought. The animals come to us as a gift from the heart of God. And He, God, is love. Surely he will do what is best for the animals."

Twenty minutes later, as Mass concluded, the entire congregation headed for the Pieta to visit with the animals. Halfway to the garden gate a sudden **Bang**, **Bang** was heard followed by a **Bang, Bang, Bang** and a flurry of animals and birds scattering in all directions. Father Mark, Charlie, and John raced to the head of the crowd and ran through the garden charging out the gate into the sunshine. Two teenage boys with rifles were seen running into the woods leaving behind two dead birds and a small black animal lying on the ground next to the Pieta. Cautiously running to the animal Charlie's heart began to sink.

"Don't let it be Aroma; please Lord, don't let it be Aroma."

THE MONK & THE SKUNK

Reaching the animal Charlie stopped, afraid to turn it over and see its face. Immediately John arrived followed by Father Mark.

"It looks like Aroma, Charlie. Should I turn it over?"

Charlie was overcome with grief and couldn't answer John as tears ran down his face. Father Mark reached down and turned the animal over.

"No! No! Aroma my friend, my good friend…why did this happen" Charlie cried as he reached out and touched his lifeless body.

"Charlie wait, he's breathing, look his eyes are opening", John shouted.

Father Mark put his hand next to three bullet holes on aromas left side.

"Charlie, John, he is bleeding profusely from three wounds."

"Charlie, I think I'm dying, I…"

"Don't try to talk Aroma, save your strength!"

"Fragrance and my two sons ran into the woods when the birds were shot and I…"

"We'll find them and bring them back Aroma, but try to rest and save your strength"

"Charlie will I go to Heaven…I feel all my strength going out of me…

"God loves you Aroma, don't worry"

As Charlie and Aroma spoke, priests, brothers, and retreatants knelt down, 60 in all, and began to pray as Aroma lay dying. Father John and Father Mark stepped aside and conferred. Suddenly John ran into the monastery.

"Charlie, will God forgive me for being unkind to Waldo? Does he forgive animals?"

"Yes my friend. God forgives you. He created you and loves you more than all of us together."

Suddenly, Father Michael and Father Gabriel emerged from the valley followed by Fragrance and her sons. Rushing to Aroma's side she hugged him and cried, 'I love you Aroma, I will always love you'.

Aroma tried to sit up but fell back down exhausted. Fragrance…I don't want to leave you, but I'm dying. I will never stop loving you… sons come closer…take care of your mother."

Father John ran from the outside garden directly to Father Mark handing him something.

"Aroma I am going to bless you with Holy Water. Be at peace, God loves you."

As Father Mark blessed Aroma his anxiety appeared to lessen.

"Fragrance I can't see clearly and I can barley breath… I love you.

Aroma seemed to lose conciseness as Fragrance hugged him and his sons moved closer. Father Mark, John and Charlie moved away to give them some privacy. Charlie was exceptionally distraught and silently knelt in prayer for Aroma. Suddenly, Fragrance screamed…"Aroma! Aroma! … Goodbye my dear husband, goodbye." Many in the crowd were visibly shaken as Aroma passed away. Their prayers and tears continued for some time.

After consultation with the staff, Father Mark announced that a funeral and burial for Aroma would take place within the hour. As preparations were being made, the birds that lived near the Monastery brought the news of the funeral to all the animals that lived in the valley. By the time the funeral was about to begin hundreds upon hundreds of animals and birds were present. A short distance from the Pieta a grave and headstone were prepared for Aroma. The headstone read:

Aroma

2005 - 2017

A devoted husband and father

He loved Jesus God

and all of His creation.

As the funeral began Charlie played Amazing Grace on his guitar while sixty people and, hundreds of animals, joined in song. It was a very emotional moment for everyone, especially Charlie. All the memories flooded back and brought many tears with them. But somehow Charlie knew that he was not the one who would suffer the most. As the funeral concluded and everyone slowly walked away he could see Fragrance and her sons reach the pathway to the valley and suddenly turn around to look back to the Pieta and Aroma's grave. Only she would feel the pain that no one else could experience. Charlie was determined to pray for her and her sons and visit them as often as needed. It was the very least he could do for his good friend Aroma.

As Charlie finished giving instructions to the workers who would lower Aroma into the grave, he then began to follow the last of the priests to the monastery. Suddenly, a familiar voice yelled, "Aroma! Aroma!" Charlie spun around to see Target flying to Aroma's grave site as the workers dropped their shovels and quickly moved away from his body.

"He's alive....He's alive" Target shouted over and over as he flew into the woods to alert the animals. Charlie rushed to Aroma's side as he slowly began to sit up and whisper... "I was sent back... God allowed me to come back. St. Francis of Assisi and many animals and humans, including Randy, pleaded with God to let me come back and live the rest of my life with my family."

As Aroma was speaking there was a stampede of animals rushing to the Monastery. In minutes a crowd of animals and humans filled the property to overflowing. Suddenly, Aroma spotted Fragrance climbing out of the valley and rushing toward him. Although he was still in shock from the miracle that had occurred, he jumped to his feet as the multitude moved aside giving him a clear path to meet her. With a flood of tears he raced toward Fragrance and in seconds they flew into each other embrace as hundreds of startled animals cheered and rejoiced at the return of their friend. Aroma asked Charlie to pick him up so he could address the gathering. The workers rushed the pulpit to Charlie's side and Charlie set him on top.

"My friends, animals and humans; Heaven is filled with all of us. Those who love, and forgive, and are kind hearted and humble are everywhere. It is such a wonderful and happy and peaceful place. And God is so gentle. When He looks at you, you are overcome with love and peace and joy. You don't want to leave him. If we want to go to Heaven then we must be like those who are there."

As Aroma continued to address the crowd Father Damian and Father Mark stepped aside and conferred.

"Father Damian, it looks like we have our work cut out for us. The last seminar in the valley had 375 animals and birds participating. Next month, for our fourth seminar, we better plan on at least 500. How do you intend to address the questions about Heaven?

"Father Mark, I have spent the last 45 years as a Theologian. All the truths that I have preached are just as I have preached them. Before I make any decisions about how I will present this new information, I'll need to get a good night's sleep. Then, tomorrow morning, I will have an in depth discussion with Aroma. Knowing that God's ways are not our ways, I will continue to seek the truth from Him in prayer. Whatever He reveals to me through His Holy Spirit, I will accept.

— — — — — — — — —

> "The Lord is good to all,
> compassionate to every creature."
>
> Psalm 145 v/s 9 NAB

At Franciscan churches, a friar with brown robe and white cord often welcomes each animal with a special prayer. The Blessing of Pets usually goes like this:

"Blessed are you, Lord God, maker of all living creatures. You called forth fish in the sea, birds in the air and animals on the land. You inspired St. Francis to call all of them his brothers and sisters. We ask you to bless this pet. By the power of your love, enable it to live according to your plan. May we always praise you for all your beauty in creation. Blessed are you, Lord our God, in all your creatures! Amen."

> *"Only the human person, created in the
> Image and likeness of God, is capable of raising
> a hymn of praise and thanksgiving to the creator.
> The earth with all its creatures and the entire universe
> call on Man to be their voice."*
>
> *Saint John Paul II*

Nothing will benefit human health and increase the chances for survival of life on Earth as much as the evolution to a vegetarian diet.
Albert Einstein

It should not be believed that all beings exist for the sake of the existence of man. On the contrary, all the other beings too have been intended for their own sakes and not for the sake of anything else.
Rabbi Moses ben Maimon (1135-1204)

If slaughterhouses had glass walls, everyone would be vegetarian. We feel better about ourselves and better about the animals, knowing we're not contributing to their pain.
Paul McCartney and Linda McCartney

Wild animals never kill for sport. Man is the only one to whom the torture and death of his fellow creatures is amusing in itself.
James A. Froude (1818-1894)

Until he extends the circle of compassion to all living things, man will not himself find peace.
Albert Schweitzer, The Philosophy of Civilization

A man can live and be healthy without killing animals for food; therefore, if he eats meat, he participates in taking animal life merely for the sake of his appetite. And to act so is immoral.
Leo Tolstoy

But where was I to start? The world is so vast, I shall start with the country I knew best, my own. But my country is so very large. I had better start with my town. But my town, too, is large. I had best start with my street. No, my home. No, my family. Never mind, I shall start with myself.
Elie Wiesel

Life is as dear to a mute creature as it is to man. Just as one wants happiness and fears pain, just as one wants to live and not die, so do other creatures.
His Holiness the Dalai Lama

Cowardice asks the question - is it safe?
Expediency asks the question - is it politic?
Vanity asks the question - is it popular?
 But conscience asks the question - is it right?
 And there comes a time when one must take a position that is neither safe, nor politic, nor popular; but one must take it because it is right.
Martin Luther King Jr.

Unless someone like you cares a whole lot, nothing is going to get better, it's not.
Dr. Seuss, The Lorax

Never doubt that a small group of thoughtful committed citizens can change the world. Indeed, it is the only thing that ever has.
Margaret Mead

About the Author
John Regan is a lover of God's creation. From raising pigeons and breeding Labradors as a young boy, to rescuing birds and animals as an adult, he eventually joined the ranks of vegetarians' to stop the slaughter of God's creatures. In his professional life John became a radio news broadcaster, television weather man, business owner, President of Network for Re-entry Prison Ministry and President of Palm Beach County Right to Life League Inc. Now, as an author, John continues to call attention to God's creation by writing *The Monk & The Skunk*, his sixth book, which follows the very popular *Return of the Children*. Married to his wife Joan for fifty one years, they live in South Florida with their three children, eight grandchildren, and two great grandchildren. John may be reached at:
johnregan2100@gmail.com

Other books by John

Heaven Who gets in and who must wait
Return of the Children
Little Bluey learns to fly

About the illustrator:
Michelle R. Morse is a muralist and illustrator who is well-known in South Florida and across the United States for her colorful and whimsical murals and children's book illustrations. She has traveled on several mission trips to Honduras to paint murals in an orphanage and teach art to the orphans. She is also the illustrator of the DVD Family Time with Santa, winner of 15 awards, the 2005 Dove Award for best children's programming, the Good Housekeeping seal of approval, and others. In addition, she is the approved muralist for the Broward County (Greater Fort Lauderdale) school system. She has two adult children, two grandchildren, and lives with her husband in Coral Springs, Florida. Contact Michelle at, jgmorse@bellsouth.net.

www.ingramcontent.com/pod-product-compliance
Lightning Source LLC
Chambersburg PA
CBHW051751040426
42446CB00007B/315